THE
BRITISH BUS
IN THE
SECOND WORLD WAR

THE BRITISH BUS IN THE SECOND WORLD WAR

JOHN HOWIE

AMBERLEY

To Bruna and Jennifer who have lived with buses for over thirty years and consequently know more about them than they ever wished to.

Frontispiece: Conductresses were essential to the industry throughout the war. This lady is in the employ of Eastern Counties. (*Gavin Booth Collection*)

First published 2013

Amberley Publishing
The Hill, Stroud
Gloucestershire, GL5 4EP

www.amberley-books.com

British Library Cataloguing in Publication Data.
A catalogue record for this book is available from the British Library.

ISBN 978 1 4456 1708 4
ebook ISBN 978 1 4456 1717 6

Typesetting and Origination by Amberley Publishing.
Printed in Great Britain.

Contents

List of Appendices

I

General Introduction

This publication originated from a treatise I wrote for a Diploma in Transport History. While researching that project it became apparent that there was a considerable amount of available information giving an insight into operating practices relating to the road passenger transport industry during the Second World War that had not previously been published.

Although the government intended to write a definitive history, and selected material was retained for this purpose, this never fully materialised but Savage's *Inland Transport* (Savage, C. I., *Inland Transport* [London: HMSO/Longman, 1957]), gives an appreciation of some of the challenges and problems of the industry during this period.

Very few individual histories of bus companies do justice to the war years, mainly due to the lack of official records and the inability of the 'casual observer' to record what he saw. However, books on London, Manchester, Wolverhampton, Liverpool and Thames Valley have particularly good coverage and give an indication of the additional problems of the times. It is not my intention to repeat detail but I have attempted to fill in some of the 'gaps' while endeavouring to give an idea of the magnitude of the additional demands and the nationwide nature of their impact over a period of seven years. Topics covered include Royal Ordnance Factories, vehicle shortages, personnel and the requirement of operators to adhere to a stream of 'endless' instructions issued by various government departments.

My main sources have, therefore, been the trade press and files still extant in The National Archive (TNA) at Kew. The former were very restricted in what they could report and the latter are far from complete; as far as I can ascertain almost no files remain of correspondence between Regional Traffic Commissioners (RTCs) and individual operators; hence, the impact on detailed day-to-day operations is difficult to fully appreciate. The Central Government files at Kew are 'random'; some contain considerable detail while others are merely general overviews. Often a topic is discussed only for the final outcome not to be recorded. This may be due to the government's limited understanding of the industry, which is evident from many of the files where problems were 'left to sort themselves out', thus begging the question of why the Ministry of War Transport (MoWT) became involved in these particular matters at all.

Consequently, I have been in a dilemma as to how much detail to include but I decided that, having extracted the information, I would include most of it and, therefore, apologise for any 'unbalanced' result this has produced. The inclusion of a few detailed examples, however, gives an indication of the scale of the total UK resources employed in meeting the demands placed upon the industry.

Despite considerable prior planning, the first few weeks of the war produced a series of problems for bus operators, starting with the evacuation of major population centres, managing 'blackout' restrictions, coping with massive personnel changes and generally taking on additional responsibilities for civil defence and other duties. After the consequential short-term readjustments, the most difficult problem in running buses during wartime was that the industry was 'continually under-resourced'. An assumption made, without any proper analysis, in 1939 that there was adequate capacity soon proved incorrect and the position worsened as additional demands were created by new government factories. Personnel recruitment and retention were difficult and supplies of new vehicles inadequate to keep up with demand, especially in the early years.

The situation became so desperate in late 1941 that the government was obliged to investigate every possible means of increasing capacity and efficiency. This led to the introduction of perimeter seating, articulated buses, re-bodying of single-deckers as doubles and, ultimately to the manufacture of the utility Guys, Daimlers and Bedfords. The search for economies in operations ranged from abolition of restrictive fare zones, curtailment of evening and Sunday services and a high-level review to see whether transport operators could be merged, to reduce overheads and 'idle vehicle' requirements. The Ministry seemed a little unsure of how to discharge its responsibilities in monitoring the bus industry and, consequently, became involved with some surprisingly detailed matters as exemplified by the 'South Wales study' and A. H. Hardcastle's fares (as will be detailed later).

Such was the shortfall in capacity that the army was forced to assist with the provision of services (using their requisitioned coaches) for a few months in early 1941. Later, once the army had been equipped with alternative personnel carriers, the intention was to release these coaches for civilian use but this did not occur as, by then, there was a growing demand for transport from the Ministry of Supply (MoS), civil defence and similar institutions; thus, most of the vehicles remained unavailable until the end of the war.

As might have been expected, the major impact on the industry occurred at the beginning of the war, after which an established pattern began to emerge. However, a steady stream of directives and instructions continued until the end of hostilities and resources remained severely constrained. I have found over 100 regulations that were additional to the normal peacetime legislation covering such aspects as vehicle construction, lighting restrictions, hours of operation, alternative fuels and passenger control. Additionally many municipal general managers were charged with

Maidstone Corporation 1943 Duple-bodied Guy (GKT 164) was a typical wartime municipal bus. (*OS/JFP*)

Withers of Bagborough operated this pre-war Dennis in the Taunton area. (*OS/JFP*)

An unusual bus comprising a Bedford QL goods chassis and the body from a small pre-war bus. Nothing more is known about (CCJ 421). (*OS/JFP*)

operation and maintenance of ARP and associated fleets of 'emergency vehicles', while all operators had to be prepared to be able to meet an 'instant demand' to transport troops or evacuees.

Viewed from sixty years on, it is difficult to imagine the massive changes to social life, particularly the role of women in society, that were inflicted by the Second World War and their impact on routine bus operations. The gradual return to civilian life, decommissioning of the factories and reabsorption of returning soldiers meant that the consequences were still being felt by the industry some five years after it finished.

Apart from the masked headlights and white edging, this Southern National Bristol (DOD 529) shows little evidence of wartime. (*OS/DHDS*)

Newport buses appear similarly unaffected by the war. (*OS/DHDS*)

2

Governmental Structure

Ministry of War Transport Regional Traffic Commissioners

As at March 1944:

Wartime Traffic Areas

Ref	Name	Office	Commissioner
1	Northern	Newcastle	Maxwell
2	North East	Leeds	Eastwood
3	Midland (North)	Nottingham	Stirk
4	Eastern	Cambridge	Faulkner
5	Metropolitan	London	Robinson
6	Southern	Reading	Piggott
7	South West	Bristol	Robinson
8	South Wales	Cardiff	Morgan
8B	North Wales	Caernarvon	Williams (from 1944)
10	North West	Manchester	Chamberlain
11	Scotland	Edinburgh	Henderson
11A	Scotland (North)	Aberdeen	Riches (1940 and 1941)

Note: Mr Chamberlain died in May 1944 and was replaced (temporarily) by C. W. Mcleod and then W E Macve.

Pettifers of Bromyard were using ex-London Transport Regal (GF 569), formerly London Transport T135. It is seen here in Hereford Bus Station (*OS/DHDS*)

A fine view of ex-City of Oxford AEC Regent (JO 1624) still looking smart with Venture of Basingstoke, despite obvious wear and tear! (*OS/DHDS*)

The RTCs reported to the Director General (Cyril Hurcombe) who, in turn, was responsible to the Minister, a post held by succession of people:

April 1939–May 1940: Captain Euan Wallace
May 1940–October 1940: Sir John Reith
October 1940–May 1941: Lt-Col. Moore-Brabazon
May 1941–July 1945: Lord Leathers (Minister of War Transport)

To address the additional complexities resulting from the war, a number of additional committees were established to support the Minister. The main ones were:

Defence (Transport) Council – heads of each of the emergency divisions of MoT.
Central Transport Committee – inter-departmental government body.
Transport Advisory Council – included industry representatives.
Inland Transport War Council –includes (non-official) industry representatives, chosen for their ability to assist MoWT in continuous plans to strengthen the department.

This picture depicts what is almost certainly the first post-war Standerwick departure from London Victoria Coach Station (RN 8658) indicating that 'normality' was returning. (*Wilf Dodds collection*)

3

Strategic Planning

Establishment of the 'Emergency Scheme'

As early as 1937 the Government produced a memorandum entitled 'Control of Road & Rail Transport in Time of War', which determined that, should hostilities commence, responsibility for the provision, allotment and coordination of all forms of transport should rest with the Minister of Transport (MoT). At the time it was envisaged that this would encompass the railway system, 500,000 goods road vehicles and 50,000 buses. The MoT was also empowered to requisition property (excluding land) according to necessity.

Following on from this decision, the administrative framework known as the 'Emergency Scheme' was set in place. Within this, the Government would exercise direct control of all road transport through Regional Traffic Commissioners (RTCs) who were effectively the same individuals who had previously acted as Traffic Commissioners but with greatly increased powers including responsibility for requisitioning vehicles for the armed forces and civil defence. To simplify administration, RTC areas were adjusted to correspond with civil defence boundaries – this saw the reintroduction of a Southern Region and the transfer of parts of North West England from Northern to North West Area. In theory, the whole operation was to be overseen by the Road Transport (Defence) Advisory Committee. However, as will be seen, the procedure did not work satisfactorily because, in practice, individual departments within government acted autonomously without regard for consequences elsewhere.

The fundamental principle was that all long-distance traffic should be carried by rail leaving the buses for local services only. This assumed adequate capacity on both modes. However, no realistic assessment had been made of either the existing fleets, in the case of the bus industry, or the impact of increased and changed demand, as a consequence of war, for either mode. As there was no overall well-defined policy and no mechanism to link demand and supply to produce coordinated transport provision, severe difficulties soon arose. The military authorities further complicated the situation by taking unilateral action in requisitioning vehicles directly from operators, thus

A Newbury & District conductor takes a rest with his Leyland Lion (HD 4371). (*OS/DHDS*)

City of Oxford (HFC 410) waits departure from Oxford for Bedford. (*OS/DHDS*)

further reducing capacity on an unplanned basis. This mismatch became very apparent in the autumn of 1940 and during the following winter resulted in a 'critical shortfall in supply'. The immediate consequence was the establishment of the Central Transport Committee (CTC) in April 1941. This inter-departmental control body had the main objective of 'achieving maximum economies in the use of transport'; one of their primary objectives being the early need to consider the optimum provision of transport to new factories and to determine between road and rail services where they were provided in parallel.

Evacuation of Major Cities

Detailed plans for evacuating children from cities were drawn up as early as May 1938 and revised frequently in the following year. The main mode of transport was to be rail, supplemented by local journeys by bus at each end. A file in Lewes Records (representative of many such schemes throughout Britain) contains a comprehensive plan drawn up in September 1938, including miscellaneous correspondence relating to the evacuation of civilians from London.

Over a period of two days, trains were planned from London to Brighton and Hove every twenty minutes, and less frequently to many other south coast stations. It was estimated that 100 vehicles (supplied by Southdown, East Kent, Maidstone &

Some elderly vehicles were still providing essential wartime services. Here is a 1929 Ford AA (RX 4367) probably in Newbury. (*OS/DHDS*)

Albion (HVX 221) of Ongar & District in wartime livery. (*OS/DHDS*)

District) would be required each day to move evacuees onwards to their destinations. The planning process was thorough, quoting the number of people to be moved to each destination and allocating the necessary resources. A contemporary report of the execution of a similar scheme in Kent states 'most scheduled trains between there and London were withdrawn for a few days: onward transport (in Kent) was provided by London Transport buses 'of all types' some having been re-licensed, after recovery from dealers'.

Throughout the country, thousands of people were moved during this short period resulting in unprecedented demands on bus companies. As well as the London programme, further recorded examples include a four day evacuation of 65,000 people from Birmingham, deploying over 400 Midland Red vehicles on each day, and Northern General using 120 vehicles over a two day-period to transport children in the Newcastle area. Many of the vehicles were hired from independent operators.

Once the children had been relocated to these 'safer' areas an immediate new transport demand was created by parents wishing to visit them. As the RTCs would not sanction extra regular services the need was met by 'private-party work'. This was deemed to be an inefficient use of resources, and consequently the RTCs were asked to establish an organised network for these services making maximum use of rail transport.

Independent operators in Horsham including a Duple-bodied Bedford (CPL 91) belonging to Ewhurst & District. (*OS/DHDS*)

Blue Coaches Dennis (OV 8100) en route to Oxford. (*OS/DHDS*)

4

The Immediate Consequences

Vehicle Lighting Restrictions

A review of the position in *Bus & Coach* (February 1941) began with the comment 'lighting regulations became operative from 1 September 1939, at only a few hours' notice, and from then onwards the position became somewhat confused largely because every policeman in the country had his own view as to whether or not a particular light was 'legal'. The requirement was that interior lights must not be visible outside the vehicle. Without any guidelines, operators responded as best they could, resulting in a number of different solutions. Methods adopted included dipping the interior light bulbs in a green or blue dye, endless varieties of metal masks and obscuring all the windows with blue paint.

Exterior headlights were only allowed to shine through a 3/8-inch slot, which necessitated masking the lamp with paint, cardboard or sheet metal, while side and tail lamps were similarly treated to give a maximum aperture of 2-inch diameter and the light diffused by the equivalent of two thicknesses of white tissue paper. Within two weeks the rules were amended – the bulb had to be removed from the offside headlamp and the nearside one had to be fitted with a cardboard disc covering so as to leave a semi-circular 2-inch aperture. Provided the lower half of the reflector was painted black, a hood was no longer required. Three weeks later the rules changed again – this time it was the offside headlamp that had to be used and an official specification mask was announced. However, when the appropriate order came into operation on 22 January 1940, either or both headlamps could be used subject to a maximum level of light emissions and route number/destination panels could be illuminated to a sufficient degree to make them readable.

By February 1941, there was still no precise definition of the amount of light permitted *inside* vehicles but the lamps had to comply with the following:

1 They must be shaded so that no part of the bulb through which the light is allowed to pass can be seen from any point outside the vehicle.

Manchester Corporation all-Leyland TD5 (FNA 346), with nearside headlamp masked, in the early days of the war. (*OS/DHDS*)

Another Manchester Corporation double-decker. This Crossley-bodied 'Mancunian' (DNB 46) has an offside headlight mask; the opposite of the Leyland pictured above. (*OS/DHDS*)

In the first few weeks of the war, lighting restrictions were subject to 'local interpretation', coastal areas being particularly sensitive. This Eastbourne AEC (JK 7428) also shows an early attempt at camouflage.

2   The illumination produced at any point at the level of any of the seats in the vehicle must not exceed 0.1 foot-candles.

3   The illumination produced at any point at ground level outside the vehicle must not exceed 0.001 foot-candles.

There was also a specification relating to platform lights.

As stated above, as there was no national directive regarding levels of interior illumination, the initiative was left to the local police, who were far from consistent in their requirements especially in coastal areas, which needed to be subject to stricter controls than many rural areas. The frustrations caused to operators are noted in their individual experiences as related elsewhere in this book.

Eastbourne Corporation took an early professional approach to meeting restrictions. Externally it moved the nearside side lamp to the tip of the mudguard wing which, suitably hooded, proved very effective. Selected windows were painted on the outside with a blue translucent paint, leaving the remaining windows fully uncovered in daytime; at night these windows were covered with blinds made of blue Rexine. The front bulkhead was already fitted with blinds but to prevent light escaping via the rear

Trolleybuses were also subject to wartime regulations (even though their fares were not) as exemplified by this Bournemouth Corporation example with headlight masks and white-painted extremities.

platform a Hessian cloth, rubberised on one side, was fitted across the lower saloon exit. Hung with rings from an iron rod, this was merely drawn across by passengers as they entered or left. The net result was a passenger environment providing a near-normal level of internal illumination to the benefit of both crew and passengers.

These measures were introduced in late 1939 but it is probable that they had to be discontinued once a new order came into force from January 1940.

Licensing Changes

The normal issue of licences for vehicles, routes and personnel was suspended and replaced by a 'defence permit system' under the comprehensive powers delegated to the RTCs. This eliminated much of the previous 'quasi-judicial procedure' as permits were issued instead of PSV licences for drivers and conductors and the necessity for a Certificate of Fitness was withdrawn as was the ability to contest services prior to their introduction. New routes were granted under a permit system (which had to be displayed on vehicles) after the RTC had contacted all affected parties.

Left: Operators were encouraged to disperse vehicles overnight in case the depot was damaged. Here a Nottingham AEC is plugged into a lamp post. (*Bus & Coach*)

Below: To reduce the risk of vehicle losses in air raids, many vehicles were parked away from their depots as exemplified by this line up of London Transport vehicles on the embankment. (*OS/EGPM*)

A close-up of a Liverpool Corporation bus 'garaged' overnight in a local park.

Use of remote parking grounds reduced the risk of damage to vehicles through air raids.

5

The First Six Months

Reports from a Selection of Municipal General Managers

The experiences of the first few months of the war were sufficiently different from normal operations to warrant considerable coverage in the Trade Press. *Passenger Transport* (13 October 1939) recorded the views of twenty-two separate municipal managers, highlighting their principal tasks and concerns. Some of the challenges had been overcome, including the successful evacuation of women and children from many cities to rural destinations, effecting building alterations and formal instructions for the protection of employees from the effect of air raids. They were also involved in revising timetables and the acceptance of additional responsibilities for ARP, ambulances and other civil defence vehicle needs. Other problems that still had to be resolved were adequate vehicle lighting to meet the blackout requirements and the absorption of a significant amount of female labour into the industry. As many of the themes were common, a few examples will give the nature of the problems:

Birmingham was overwhelmed with applicants once it had announced it intended to recruit women (at the same pay rates as men). However, fuel rationing led to the immediate curtailment of services, hence they were not required.

The lack of a 'national standard' for vehicle lighting in the blackout meant that it was subject to the whims of individual policemen and wardens. The general manager took it upon himself to agree a policy directly with the deputy chief constable.

Bolton assisted with evacuations from Manchester, converted some buses into temporary ambulances, had problems achieving satisfactory vehicle lighting, considered female conductors and decided to retain the remainder of the tramway system to conserve fuel supplies.

At **Bury,** the GM stated that he had been ordered to concentrate on civil defence matters, even at the expense of normal bus operations. He was worried about the

An excellent wartime photograph of a Midland Red SOS. This make of vehicle was of no interest to the military authorities. (*OS/CFK*)

financial effect of additional war-related costs as no indication had been agreed as to how these would be recovered.

Leicester had reorganised some routes so that buses fed into tram routes. It was also worried about cost reimbursement.

At **London Transport** the main impact had been the withdrawal of all Green Line routes.

Manchester had instigated staff training schemes for first aid, anti-gas and fire-fighting. The department was now responsible for over 900 extra vehicles engaged on ARP, ambulance and civil defence duties. Additional services were required to government factories, and vehicle cleaning and maintenance had been transferred from nights to days.

A joint Industrial Council of Emergency had been set up with the trade unions, which it was hoped would speed up the resolution of any staff-related matters.

Rochdale was considering the reduction in the number of stopping places to reduce vehicle wear and fuel consumption. It was noted that there had been an increase in traffic caused by visitors to the evacuees in the area.

GH889 and another ex-London Leyland (TD class) are seen when operating for 'Green, Brierley Hill' in wartime attire'. (*Roy Marshall collection*)

A Green Line coach about to leave London Victoria for East Grinstead. All such services were withdrawn after September 1942. (*OS/EGPM*)

Rotherham found it had surplus staff even after the timetable adjustments and the increased tram and trolleybus services.

Reading increased traffic due to evacuees in the area and relocation of government departments from London.

St Helens noted that their trolleybuses were not subject to cuts.

A later report in May 1940 from **Nottingham** gives an indication as to the situation nine months after the declaration of war. Here, there was a continual revision of schedules as the days got longer, hence less time to operate in blackout conditions, a position that was eased by advancing the commencement of Summer Time to 25 February. It was noted that the difficult winter conditions had led to very high sickness levels.

Route changes included using trams and trolleybuses as 'feeders' to buses wherever possible and reaching agreements to allow company buses to pick up passengers within the city boundaries when space was available. All these measures were designed to obtain maximum vehicle utilisation.

Professional help (from the university) had been sought to successfully resolve the 'lighting problem'.

A major worry was the worsening financial situation as the extra costs had not been covered by revenue increases; there was concern at the increasing number of

An unusual bus comprising a Bedford QL goods chassis and the body from a small pre-war bus. Nothing more is known about CCJ 421. (*OS/JFP*)

A wartime view of Haymond of Wonersh, with a locally built Dennis BPK 617, in Guildford. (*OS/JFP*)

A distinctive Northern SE6 model (CN 6103) on a local service around Gateshead. (*OS*)

A typical wartime view of a United Counties Bristol (VV 8252). (*OS/CFK*)

workman's fares being issued, advertising revenue had reduced and spare parts were becoming more expensive as stocks reduced.

Edinburgh took action from 1 September to 'darken' offices and depots and ran buses on sidelights only until approval for improvised headlight screening was obtained. Most interior lights were removed with the remainder fitted with cardboard shields. Trams had their bumpers and stairs painted white but interior lights were fitted with blue bulbs rather than being removed. Blue lacquer was applied to destination boxes and brake and platform lights removed. Within a few months, however, lighting circuits on most trams were modified enabling the use of normal bulbs with cardboard shades.

As at other locations, employees were trained in ARP duties including 'decontamination' procedures. A purpose-built unit was built to accommodate trams and/or buses should the need arise.

6

'An Impending Crisis' and Military Assistance

Demand Exceeds Supply

The bus industry appeared to adapt well to its changed circumstances with no significant problems during the first year of war. However, a combination of developing trends of reduced supply and increased demand proved too much for some operators; the resultant lack of adequate transport in some regions began to have an effect on the output of war materials. The matter was so serious it was brought to the attention of the War Cabinet. The main contributing factors to the problem were identified as the construction of 'remote' factories, with the corresponding reduced efficiency in transport utilisation, the increase in 'peak' traffic where factories had expanded to increase output, the need to provide services to remote military camps and the withdrawal of fuel for private motoring. On the supply side, over 4,000 buses and coaches had been diverted to military and government use.

Winter 1941/2

By December 1941 it was becoming apparent that there were insufficient resources within the industry to meet demand during the current winter. At discussions of the House of Lord's President's Committee, the Minister of Labour (MoL) became concerned that lack of transport was 'impeding wartime production'.

The following recorded observations indicate the thinking at that time:

1   The 500 vehicles held in 'reserve' should be brought into use and all 'pleasure trips' (which had been a legitimate use until then) be curtailed due to public criticism.
2   It was estimated that 6,000 new buses per year were required but noted that only 500 (reduced from original 1,000) were scheduled for 1942. The MoS was asked to 'make every effort to meet MoWT requirements for new vehicles'.
3   A decision was taken not to proceed with the production of 500 articulated buses.

Southdown CCD 940 in its wartime livery. Note the 'No Entry' sign on the shop wall and the 'homemade blinds'! (*OS/CFK*)

Crosville KA 121 (DFM 332), a 1939 ECW-bodied Leyland TS8 en route to Chester. (*BCVM*)

4   The request for 1,200 single-deck vehicles for delivery from June 1942 was supported.

5   It was noted that the Admiralty only had fifty buses under its control.

6   The army was gradually replacing its buses with purpose-built troop carriers and hoped to be able to release 800 coaches, by the end of 1941, for civilian use under the control of MoWT.

7   The army were willing to lend seven Military Coach Companies (420 vehicles) for civilian use during December 1941 and January 1942. It was, however, suggested that some might not be useable without major maintenance.

8   The RAF had 700 buses of their own plus 350 on hire – it was hoped to be able to release the latter in 4–5 months' time.

9   There were also three RAF Motor Transport companies (each with thirty-two buses) but these were fully utilised. However, commanding officers were to be asked to make any surplus available for civilian use for transport of factory workers.

10 Most factory shifts were now 'staggered' to reduce resources.

11 It was suggested that as more vehicles became available there would be a shortage of drivers and the MoL was asked to create 'driver pools' and control their allocation.

12 It was noted that a 'pooling' arrangement of transport resources operated to support the South Wales coal mines and it was suggested that a similar scheme be introduced in County Durham.

13 Concern was expressed regarding a scheme using hired buses, operating in Coventry, that was not considered to be an economical use of resources.

Many of the above did not materialise as the military authorities did not release vehicles as quickly as the above predictions and when they did become available they were reallocated to other government departments and Royal Ordnance factories (ROFs) by the Ministry of Supply and were, thus, unavailable for general civilian use. However, the Army did operate a considerable number of civilian services during the 1941/2 winter.

The Requisitioning Process in Detail

The War Office became one of the largest coach operators as it realised the advantages of such vehicles for both large- and small-scale troop movements.

At the start of the war the larger companies were instructed to keep a number of vehicles on stand by for army use, while similar arrangements were made with small proprietors whose vehicles would otherwise be out of use for the winter. The actual use made of these facilities is not recorded but it was not uncommon for vehicle and driver to be away from their base for a number of days when transporting troops. Photographic evidence shows that individual vehicles even reached France.

After Dunkirk the army decided it needed the flexibility of operating its own vehicles. This led to a rapid requisitioning of coaches from a large number of operators under the 'Emergency Powers (Defence), Acquisition & Disposal of Motor Vehicles Order (1940)'.

Requisitions were initially authorised under the Army Acts but from July 1940 responsibility passed to the Regional Transport Commissioner. Army officers still took the vehicles but the RTC was *supposed* to advise on the most suitable, given his responsibility to ensure local transport needs were met as effectively as possible. Compensation was either agreed on the spot or via a formal claims procedure. No account was taken of the fact that vehicle prices generally had increased significantly due to the war and most settlements were based on the price at which the vehicle last changed hands.

Companies had varying degrees of success in hiding their prime vehicles from the requisitioning officers, Thames Valley being one of the lucky ones. However, those that were required were taken (by military drivers) to Aldershot and either allocated to

A series of posed pictures which shows requisitioned coaches in use 'on army manoeuvres'. This one is of either Bristol or Dennis manufacture.

Army Manoeuvres 2 – an unidentified requisitioned Leyland.

Army Manoeuvres 3 – another view of the same Leyland.

Army Manoeuvres 4 – and another.

the No. 7 Motor Coach Company or, if not needed by the military, to No. 1 Vehicle Collection Centre from where they were allocated to ordnance factories or for use overseas; a process that was repeated throughout the UK.

In late 1941 it is estimated that about 6,700 vehicles had been commandeered to date. Normally only minimal alterations were made, including application of camouflage paint, replacement of windows with metal sheeting or canvas screens and modification to reduce lighting to a minimum but instances are known where vehicles were fitted with guns.

Use of Army Coaches

In November 1941, the War Office asked the Ministry of War Transport whether the use of army coaches (with drivers) during December 1941 and January 1942 would be of any help for civilian transport but, by the time the MoWT had asked the Regional Traffic Commissioners who in turn asked operators and got replies, it was January 1942 before any vehicle started work. As can be determined from the detailed reports that follow, once employed they made a significant impact in many areas of the country.

The Regional Transport Commissioner for Wales submitted a report summarising the situation in his area:

Left: CV 5329 is a survivor from the time when village proprietors had their own small bus. This Surrey Dodge dates from 1931. (*OS/DHDS*)

Below: Carpenters of Bishop's Castle; Daimler VD 1524, originally new to CSMT. (*OS/CFK*)

Two interesting vehicles of Vagg, Knockin Heath, meet in the traditional manner of a country operator. (*OS/CFK*)

The coaches commenced operation on Monday 5 January. The majority are being employed on workers services where additional transport facilities are required and others are being used in order to permit operators to overhaul their vehicles. This latter facility is greatly appreciated, as many operators have been unable to properly maintain their vehicles for some months. Operators have rendered 'every assistance' to this scheme and have welcomed the facilities, which it offers. They have also placed their available garage facilities at the disposal of the Repairs Officer of the army unit and the whole of the arrangements have been very satisfactory.

It is expected that constructional work at several factories will decrease towards the end of March and this will then free vehicles for additional services, which will be required when production commences. If the army coaches are withdrawn at the end of January, there will be difficulty in providing the necessary services and it should be pointed out that the vehicles which are now being overhauled by operators are unlikely to be ready for service at the end of the month owing to difficulty in obtaining spare parts and shortage of mechanics.

Weather conditions in this region during the next two months are likely to cause further difficulties in operating services, particularly in the Rhondda and similar valleys and the blackout period has already reduced the number of vehicles through accident.

It is therefore hoped that this application for the extension of the period of loan, to the end of March will be approved.

The 11th Motor Coach Company is now in this region with a total of 51 coaches allocated as follows:

16 at Pontypridd with Rhondda Transport Co.
10 at Newport with Red & White
9 at Bridgend with Western Welsh
4 at Pembroke Dock with W&L Silcox
4 at Carmarthen with Western Welsh
4 at Trecwn with Western Welsh
4 at Haverfordwest with Green's Motors

Report from North East Regional Traffic Commissioner (dated 9 January 1942)

The scheme is now fully in operation and working satisfactorily and some temporary relief of transport problems have been effected. With regard to the period of loan, however, it is pointed out that the vehicles loaned to this region are all engaged on aerodrome construction services and that the workmen employed by contractors can work during the period of daylight only. There were also twenty vehicles employed on internal transport duties at Royal Ordnance Factory Aycliffe.

The West Yorkshire Road Car Co. and West Riding Automobile Co. have each one platoon of army vehicles based at York and Castleford respectively and desire to retain the use of the vehicles for a period after 31 January 1942. It is, therefore, desired that you will raise the question of extending the period of loan with the War Office, as it is my view that until the period of daylight lengthens, the operators concerned will not be in a position to provide the services required from their own resources.

With regard to the vehicles based at Bridlington, a different consideration arises. These vehicles have been obtained in order to enable local operators to repair and re-condition their vehicles and the question as to whether the army vehicles should be retained depends largely on the circumstances prevailing at the end of the month. It is hoped, however, that the local operators will have carried out the necessary repairs before the end of January, but in case there is any failure in this respect I would be glad if you would endeavour to obtain authority provisionally to extend the period of loan of the vehicles based at Bridlington. It will, of course, be possible to state nearer the time whether it is in fact actually necessary to retain the vehicles. [A report in *Passenger Transport* 16 January 1942 suggests that the main reason for the hire was lack of crews and that up to 100 buses in this region were permanently out of use because of this.]

Army vehicles have arrived in Sheffield today and they will be put into service as soon as possible. It is anticipated that these vehicles will be required at least until the end of February and it is desired, therefore, that you will obtain authority for their retention at Sheffield for a further period.' [There was also a note from the General Manager of Sheffield Corporation to the RTC stating that one platoon was being used on both contract and stage-carriage services with Corporation conductors. He had refitted two vehicles with windows and bell-pushes and wondered whether it was worth spending money on the others.]

Summary of Observations from Other Areas

North West Area

Twenty-six coaches were sent to Liverpool Corporation depots at Carnegie Road and Green Lane, for the conveyance of military firewatchers to and from various points in Liverpool in order to release thirteen trams at peak periods.

Scottish Area

One platoon with Western SMT at Kilmarnock and another with Young's Bus Service, Paisley on contract services; ten vehicles with Glasgow Corporation, Knightswood garage on Ordnance Factory work (Corporation will find conductors); ten vehicles with [Central] SMT at Motherwell on workers services between Lanarkshire and Glasgow (Company will find conductors).

Western Area

One platoon at Bath on workers' stage services to Corsham (Bath Tramways conductors). [This is to enable Bath Tramways Motor Co. to convert some single-deck buses to standee configuration]

North Midlands Area

Two vehicles with T. J. Lovell & Sons Ltd, RAF Station Langar from and three vehicles with Messrs Mowlem, ROF. Ruddington : all operated by Barton Transport from 1/1/42. Three vehicles with Messrs Mowlem, ROF. Ruddington , one vehicle with LNER (East Leake Contract) and one vehicle with Bosworth & Co. (Builders) Gunthorpe, (Gunthorpe Contract): all operated by Trent from 2/1/42. Five vehicles on stage carriage services to Ordnance Factory, Sinfin Lane, Derby from 5/1/42. [Operated by Derby Corporation – factory to supply conductors] The agreement was for vehicles to operate until 25/2/42 in all cases.

West Midlands Area

A memo dated 24 January 1942 stated that two sections of Motor Transport companies would be sent to Stoke on Trent for work until 28 February with Potteries Motor Traction Co. on services to Royal Ordnance Factory, Swynnerton. All forty vehicles were returned to the Army on 27 February but ten returned to PMT on 5 March, staying until 31 March.

A Motor Coach Company consisted of three platoons. Each platoon had twenty coaches (eighteen operational and two in reserve). Files in TNA suggest there were thirty-nine MCCs, thus giving a total vehicle complement of 2,340 coaches. Presumably all these vehicles ran without registrations as the military did not retain any record of these.

Disposal from Military Service

After 1942 army coaches were gradually replaced by purpose-built vehicles and a disposal scheme was introduced. The process was extremely slow and by April 1943, the delay in reintroducing the vehicles to civilian use was causing problems. The rules stated that the original owner was allowed first choice as to whether to buy them back but many had lost their identity which led to a consequential delay while this was established. When finally offered, the vehicle was often refused as it either needed excessive maintenance or there was no longer a requirement. To speed up the process it was suggested that once a coach had been rejected by two operators it should be offered to its manufacturer but there is no evidence of this happening, as most manufacturers were engaged on war work and in no position to work on buses.

How canvas screens are used in place of the usual windows on an Army coach.

The state of many vehicles when released by the military – most needed considerable work before they could be returned to service. (*Bus & Coach*)

A few returned to civilian use at this time but the scheme was short-lived as other government departments such as Civil Defence and Ministry of Supply quickly snapped up these vehicles to meet their transport needs. Additionally, a large number of coaches had found their way to Ireland as part of the defence arrangements, in case the enemy were to use this route to launch an attack on Britain. By 1942 this was no longer seen as a threat and, rather than return all the vehicles to the mainland, 129 were purchased by the Northern Ireland Road Transport Board, who were forced to operate many of them, initially without glass in their windows as spares were almost impossible to obtain. After the war some were re-bodied as double-deckers; a few lasting until the 1960s.

Northern Ireland was not immune from the requirement to apply wartime markings to vehicles as this NIRTB Leyland, at Bangor, demonstrates. (*OS/DHDS*)

Another view at Bangor NIRTB; this one shows AEC Regal (EZ 1752) in its wartime guise. (*OS/DHDS*)

JJ 1269 was ex-London Transport TD98 which was sold (with most of the other former 'pirate' buses) to Millburn (DLR) in 1940. Purchased by McGill, Barrhead, it was fitted with an ex-Glasgow Corporation Cowieson body and is seen awaiting custom in deserted Paisley. (*OS/DHDS*)

Other Uses

Besides losing vehicles to the military and reserving others as ambulances, bus fleets saw further depletion with transfers as ancillary vehicles for other war-associated functions. Hence, while some were converted as canteens (Wallasey, Blackpool, Ashton), others performed Air Raid Precaution duties (Leigh, Derby, Chesterfield); a Brighton vehicle became a 'gunnery school' and Huddersfield provided two mobile theatres.

Sometimes bodies were separated from their chassis and the latter used for other purposes. Millburn Motors, the Glasgow dealer, was advertising in 1943: 'large number of high-class all metal thirty-two seat bus and coach bodies, removed from chassis used for emergency purposes'.

7

Difficulties Increase

Pressure on the RTCs

The Regional Transport Commissioners, being responsible for the day-to-day control of the industry, had to maintain a working relationship with the operators while implementing government directives, which, in many cases, were contrary to traditional custom and practice.

The agenda of their meetings and annual conference indicate the range of topics that fell within their remit. In January 1942 they were discussing workers' services, carriage of standing passengers, the requisitioning of premises, renewal of permits for PSV operators and the proposed discontinuation of badges for PSV drivers and conductors. They addressed the difficulties of allocating reconditioned ex-army vehicles given the problem that, of 14,300 vehicles (including goods) returned by the War Office, only 800 complied with the procedure that gave the original operator 'first refusal'. Also debated were the manpower pressures within the industry, a survey of the efficiency of regional bus resources, the shortcomings of a recent census which did not show vehicles that were idle 'due lack of labour'.

By the end of the following year the agenda had increased to include the shortage of tyres, the need to provide additional vehicles and incentives to encourage greater use of producer-gas-powered vehicles.

The RTCs were constantly under pressure from the government to supply information and impose policies on bus operators. In early 1942 a list of items currently being actioned included the need to standardise pay and conditions for bus maintenance workers, furnishing returns on the number of 'idle buses', 'spot checking' the number of buses actually required for service, encouraging operators to speed up the introduction of perimeter seating and producer-gas propulsion and addressing vehicle-maintenance problems.

Just how much power and influence they were able to exert is highlighted by the fact that the North Western Area Commissioner was able to instigate significant coordination between operators in the Liverpool area. Regarded as being one of the

Opposite above: One of West Monmouth's famous Leyland Bull buses, before starting another gruelling wartime journey up Bargoed Hill. (*OS/ CFK*)

Opposite below: These were later joined by a modified Leyland Beaver (AAX 27); pictured here en route. (*OS/CFK*)

Right: Note that the fittings have been completely removed from the nearside headlight of this Southern National AEC Regal (GJ 9036). In the early days of the war the absence of a published standard resulted in individual operators applying different strategies to meet the reduced light specifications. (*OS/ DHDS*)

more innovative, he devised emergency plans that put Liverpool Corporation (LCPT) in charge of operational requirements arising from air raids, rail disruption and other incidents, while he acted as a liaison. He arranged that LCPT was able to draw upon resources from Wallasey and Birkenhead corporations plus coaches from independent operators. The latter were arranged through the 'NWTA PSV Operators Emergency Group', which was controlled through Yelloway Motor Services of Rochdale. Such was the level of cooperation that, when required, Yelloway seconded a traffic clerk to LCPT and their coaches were housed in Liverpool depots.

The RTC also tried to ensure that all private operators received their 'fair share' of any business arising from these emergencies and the existence of these voluntary groupings helped in reaching agreement with trade unions regarding drivers forced to undertake unusual duties. One positive outcome was that drivers were often employed at factories during the long layover period between transporting workers.

Express Services and Tours Severely Restricted

The early months of the war had a mixed effect on express services and tours. The September 1939 reduction in fuel allocation caused nearly all private hire to be withdrawn immediately as well as many express services. In some cases revised services were substituted where the express had been the only transport in an area, an example being Ribble in East Lancashire. As fuel supplies became further restricted RTCs demanded further reductions; all limited stop within the jurisdiction of the North West Commissioner (excepting specific exemptions) ceased from June 1940 and only two Thames Valley express routes remained after this date. Similarly private hire and excursions ceased through lack of fuel. There was a slight easing of the supply position in the next few months allowing some leisure operation during the summer, but the position worsened again during the winter. By March 1941 the MoWT was recommending further economies but did not, at that stage, want to withdraw the remaining express services 'until drivers or vehicles were required elsewhere'. The logic was to retain a 'strategic transport reserve' in case of major difficulties on the railways.

A *Transport World* feature on Victoria Coach Station, in April 1941, confirmed that substantial operations continued. Coaches were leaving 'for most parts of England and Wales' at approximately fifteen-minute intervals, with Scottish connections available at Newcastle; thirty-five companies were represented and there were 253 coaches per weekday rising to 445 at weekends. These compared with pre-war figures of 1,250 and 2,100 respectively.

Although pleasure and holiday services were suspended there were many departures of vehicles under contract to government departments, armed forces and large commercial firms, reflecting the relocation of personnel away from London.

ARP cover was provided by station administrative staff, thus reducing any delays caused by air raid alerts, and the absence of night departures reduced risks further. Most operation was between 7.00 a.m. and 7.00 p.m. with departures timed to enable them to complete most of their journeys in daylight.

From September 1942 RTCs were made responsible for the allocation of fuel to bus operators and, at the same time, instructions were given to cease all express operations from 1 October. They remained curtailed for the rest of the war until 26 June 1945 when approval was given for leisure travel to resume. The initial limit was up to 70 miles but this restriction was lifted from 14 April 1946. Cross-country express services were also gradually reintroduced from June 1945 but it was not until mid-1946 that the network returned to the pre-war level.

Above: Keswick–Preston was one of the few express services that continued in operation throughout the war. RN 7590 is seen here in Lancaster but, strangely, showing 'Liverpool' as its destination.

Right: Most operators issued special wartime timetables. This is the cover of a Ribble example.

RIBBLE
MOTOR SERVICES LTD.

NATIONAL
**EMERGENCY
TIME TABLE**

**STAGE CARRIAGE
SERVICES**

**No. 4
SOUTH LANCS. AREA**
(Liverpool, Southport, Chorley, Wigan, Ormskirk, Bolton, &c.)

★ **Sept. 15th, 1941, to June 26th, 1942**
(INCLUSIVE)

★ All Services and Period of Operation liable to alteration, including SUSPENSION OF LATE AND LAST BUSES. Passengers are advised to enquire at Local Offices.

PRICE . . . Id.

Service 51. LIVERPOOL (St. John's Lane) and FORD CEMETERY.

(Joint Service with Liverpool Corporation Passenger Transport Department).

☛ SATURDAYS.

															then every 30 minutes until		
Liverpool, St. John's Lane ..dep.	....	....	....	....	740	8 5	840	9 5	9 42	1012	1042	1112	1142		9 12	1012
Jt.Bedford Rd.&H'thorne Rd. ,,	....	....	....	....	751	816	851	916	9 53	1023	1053	1123	1153		9 23	1023
Marsh Lane Island ,,	....	....	....	7†31	756	821	856	921	9 58	1028	1058	1128	1158		9 28	1028
Jt.H'thorne Rd.&Staley St ,,	6 26	6†40	6†55	7†10	758	823	858	923	10 0	1030	1058	1130	12 0		9 30	1030
Ford Cemetery ....arr.	6 33	6 45	7 0	7 15	8 5	830	9 5	930	10 7	1037	11 7	1137	12 7		9 37	1037

															then every 30 mins. until			
Ford Cemetery ....dep.	6 35	6 50	7 5	7 15	740	8 15	840	9 12	9 42	1012	1042	1112	1142	1217	8 47	9 12	9 47
Jt.H'thorne Rd.&Staley St ,,	6†40	6†55	7†10	7 22	7 47	8 22	8 49	9 19	9 49	1019	1049	1119	1154	1224	8 54	9 19	9 54
Marsh Lane Island ,,			7 24	7 49	8 24	8 51	9 21	9 51	1021	1051	1121	1156	1226	8 56	9 56
Jt.Bedford Rd.&H'thorne Rd. ,,			7 29	7 54	8 29	8 54	9 26	9 56	1026	1056	1126	12 1	1231	9 1	10 1
L'pool,St.John's Ln.(Lime St.) arr.	7 40	8 5	8 40	9 5	9 37	10 7	11 7	12 7	1212	1242	9 12	1012

☛ SUNDAYS.

			then every 30 minutes until
Liverpool,St.John'sln.(LimeSt)dep	....	1 12	
Jt.Bedford Rd.&H'thorne Rd. ,,	....	1 23	
Marsh Lane Island ,,	....	1 28	
Jt.H'thorne Rd.&Staley St ,,	12 3	1 0	1 30
Ford Cemetery ....arr.	1210	1 7	1 37

					then every 30 minutes until		
Ford Cemetery ....dep.	1212	1242	5 42	6 12	6 40	9 12	1012
Jt.H'thorne Rd &Staley St... ,,	1219	1249	5 49	6 19	6 47	9 19	1019
Marsh Lane Island ,,	1221	1251	5 51	6 21	6†49	9 21
Jt.Bedford Rd.&H'thorne Rd. ,,	1226	1256	5 56	6 26		9 26
Liverpool,St.John'sln.(LimeSt)arr.	1237	1 7	6 7	6 37		9 37

† Runs to or from Litherland Canal Bridge only.   ‡ Runs to or from Merton Road, 1 minute further.

☛ BLACK-OUT ☜ Services subject to slight alteration during black-out period.

59

RIBBLE
MOTOR SERVICES LTD.

Curtailment of Sunday Services
AND
Late Facilities on Mons. to Sats.
—— SKIPTON DISTRICT ——

FROM SATURDAY, NOVEMBER 7th, 1942,

at the direction of the Ministry of War Transport, on certain services in Skipton District, facilities will be curtailed on Sundays in addition to late facilities on Mondays to Saturdays as follows :—

Service	From	To	MONS. TO SATS. Last Departures, p.m.	SUNDAYS (No Morning Services) Revised Services, p.m.
250†	SKIPTON	INGLETON	5-30, 8✳40	2-30 & 5-30
	SKIPTON	SETTLE	8-40	1-30, 2-30, 5-30, 7-30 & 8-40
	SKIPTON	GARGRAVE	8-40	1-30, 2-30. 5-30, 6-30, 7 30 & 8-40
	INGLETON	SKIPTON	6-58 (10✳13 to Settle only)	3-58 & 6-58
	SETTLE	SKIPTON	7-35 (8✳35 to Hellifield only)	1-35, 2-35, 4-35, 5-35 & 7-35
	GARGRAVE	SKIPTON	8-11, 8✳15, 8✳55	2-11, 3-11, 5-11, 6.11, 7-11 & 8-11
210†	SKIPTON	MALHAM	6-0	} No service
	MALHAM	SKIPTON	6-43	
S6	SKIPTON	EASTBY	8-0	} No service
	EASTBY	SKIPTON	8-15	
	SKIPTON	EMBSAY	8-50	1-0, 3-0, 5-0, 7-0 & 8-30
	EMBSAY	SKIPTON	9K0, 9G36	1-20, 3-20, 5-20, 7-20 & 8-45
296	SKIPTON	CLITHEROE	7-9	4-9 & 7-9
	CLITHEROE	SKIPTON	5-54	2-54 & 5-54
S1	SKIPTON, (Caroline Sq.)	SKIPTON (Broughton Rd. Co's. Gar.)	8-32, 9✳0	1-32, 3-32, 4-9, 5-32, 7-9, 7-32 & 9-0
	SKIPTON (Broughton Rd. Co's. Gar.)	SKIPTON, (Caroline Sq.)	9✳51, 10-1	12-55, 2-23, 3-56, 4-23, 6-23, 6-56, 8-23 & 9-51
294†‡	COLNE	GISBURN	7-35	1-35, 3-35, 5-35 & 7-35
	COLNE	BARNOLDSWICK	9-0	1-35, 3-35, 5-35, 7-35 & 9-0
	GISBURN	COLNE	8-19	2-19, 4-19, 6-19 & 8-19
	BARNOLDSWICK	COLNE	8-35, 9-30	2-35, 4-35, 6-35, 8-35 & 9-30
228	The 9-18 p.m. journey, STANDING STONE GATE—BURNLEY, will operate DAILY (Suns exc) instead of Mons. to Fris. only.			
39†	The 10✳40 p.m. journey, LOWER BENTHAM—INGLETON will be CANCELLED.			

† Jointly with Pennine Motor Services. ✳—Saturdays only.
‡ „ „ Burnley, Colne and Nelson Joint Transport Committee.
K—Tues., Thurs., Fris., and Sats. only. G—Mons., Weds. and Sats. only.

HEAD OFFICE : FRENCHWOOD AVENUE, PRESTON. Phone 4272 (7 lines).

142/42H 3M
2/11/42 **WAR SAVINGS ARE WAR WEAPONS.**

Above: Throughout the war there were increasing restrictions on the hours of bus operation. This Ribble details those for the Skipton area from November 1942.

Opposite page: And a typical timetable page which refers to the 'blackout'.

RIBBLE MOTOR SERVICES LTD. —JOINT SERVICE— **J. FISHWICK & SONS**

COMMENCING FRIDAY, JANUARY 1st, 1943,

FIXED STOPPING PLACES

WILL BE INTRODUCED IN THE

LEYLAND URBAN DISTRICT,

CHURCH LANE and COOTE LANE, FARINGTON,

and REVISED in

CROSTON ROAD, FARINGTON

at points to be indicated by "Bus Stop" signs as described below :—

LEYLAND.

1. **LEYLAND LANE, SLATER LANE, SCHOOL LANE, and DUNKIRK LANE.**

   Outward :—Opp. Wheat Sheaf Inn ; 40 yds. from Earnshaw Bridge ; opp. Free Street ; opp. Co-op. Stores ; Nr. Old Original Seven Stars Inn ; Nr. Southlands Drive ; Nr. St. James' Church ; 40. yds. from Slater Lane ; Nr. Black Bull Inn.

   Inward :—Nr. Black Bull Inn ; Nr. Paradise Lane ; opp. Dunkirk Works ; Nr. Bowling Terrace ; Nr. Cowling Lane ; Nr. Free Street ; opp. St. John's School ; Nr. Wheatsheaf Inn.

2. **LEYLAND LANE (South of Fox Lane End).**

   40 yds. from Fox Lane ; Nr. Wade Brook Bridge.

3. **FOX LANE.**

   Nr. Forestway ; Nr. Lower House Farm.

4. **PRESTON ROAD, CHAPEL BROW, HOUGH LANE, WATER STREET, TOWNGATE, CHURCH ROAD, HEALD HOUSE ROAD and WIGAN ROAD.**

   Outward :—Opp. Railway Inn ; Nr. Telephone Kiosk ; opp. Gas Works ; Nr. Grundy's ; opp. St. Mary's Hall ; Nr. Baron's Auction Mart ; Nr. War Memorial ; opp. Balshaw's Grammar School (West Gate) ; Nr. Bent Bridge ; Nr. New Inn Corner ; "Leyland Gate."

   Inward :—"Leyland Gate" ; Nr. New Inn Corner ; Nr. Bent Bridge ; Nr. Balshaw's Grammar School (West Gate) ; Nr. Eagle & Child Inn ; Nr. Baron's Auction Mart ; Nr. St. Mary's Hall ; Nr. Ward's ; Nr. Gas Works ; Nr. District Bank ; Nr. Railway Inn.

5. **TURPIN GREEN LANE and BENT LANE.**

   Nr. Methodist Church ; Nr. Canberra Road ; Nr. Turpin Green Bridge ; Nr. Russell Avenue ; Nr. Bent Bridge (outward in Heald House Road, inward in Bent Lane).

6. **GOLDEN HILL LANE.**

   Nr. Billiard Hall ; Nr. Fishwick's Yard ; Nr. Northbrook Road ; 40 yds. from Leyland Lane.

7. **MOSS LANE.**

   Nr. Railway Station ; Nr. St. Ambrose Church.

FARINGTON.

1. **CHURCH LANE.**

   Hillside Avenue ; 30 yds. South of Coote Lane.

2. **COOTE LANE.**

   30 yds. east of School Lane ; 30 yds. West of Leyland Road.

3. **CROSTON ROAD.**

   Hugh Lane (Leyland Boundary) ; Mill Lane ; South of Sunset Bungalow ; Nr. Stanley House ; 100 yds. south of Lodge Lane ; Bamber's Stores ; 30 yds. south of Farington Cross Roads ; Farington Station ; Anchor Inn.

RIBBLE MOTOR SERVICES, Ltd.,	J. FISHWICK & SONS,
Head Office: Frenchwood Avenue,	Golden Hill, LEYLAND.
Phone 4272 (7 lines). PRESTON.	Phone 81207.

159/42H.   3M.   24/12/42.

To reduce the demand for resources, operators were required to restrict the number of stopping places as per this Ribble poster effective from 1 January 1943 and applicable to the urban district of Leyland.

8

An Urgent Need for Additional Capacity

Utility Buses

Along with the rest of manufacturing, the bus construction industry became increasingly involved in production of items essential for the war effort, resulting in a gradual slowing down in vehicle output. Some chassis and body builders ceased immediately on the outbreak of war but most continued limited production in parallel with military vehicles with deliveries becoming increasing erratic until effectively ceasing by the end of 1940.

Stocks of materials and incomplete vehicles, together with undeliverable export orders, became the responsibility of the Ministry of Supply, which released them to selected manufacturers for completion. The resultant buses and trolleybuses (generally referred to as 'unfrozen') were allocated to operators with the greatest need; thus, some unusual makes appeared in previously standardised fleets. A status report indicates that 'frozen stocks' amounted to 387 double-deck, of which 325 had been allocated to operators by September 1942. Corresponding figures for single-deck showed a total of ninety, with sixty-five allocated. 'Frozen' trolleybuses comprised ten s/d and 112 d/d.

Once all the body parts had been used up, future double-deck supplies were based on a standard utility specification vehicle, the plans for which were drawn up by the MoS and MoWT in cooperation with the National Federation of Vehicle Traders. The complete body required 1,200 fewer hours to construct than a conventional unit, as it had considerably fewer components. Its main features were:

1   Seating capacity to be either fifty-six (thirty/twenty-six) for the high-bridge version or fifty-three (twenty-seven/twenty-eight) for the low-bridge equivalent.
2   Framing to be of oak, ash, mahogany or teak – longitudinal rails could be pine.
3   Exterior panelling (including roof) to be of 20-gauge SWG steel, shaped but not beaten.
4   No interior side lining panels permitted.
5   Upper saloon emergency exit to be panelled, not glazed.

An 'unfrozen' AEC Regent with utility body is seen in SMT service in Edinburgh. (*AEC Gazette*)

Typical of the 'unfrozen' buses is this AEC allocated to Midland Red; a company with no previous examples of this marque. GHA 797 has Brush bodywork. The wartime posters on the wall relate to 'Scabies' and 'The Sick Need Your Help'. (*OS/CFK*)

Above: Ribble employed this Northern Counties 'utility' bodied Guy in Carlisle. Note the limited number of opening windows, grey livery, minute sidelights, masked headlights, white edging and the 'British Buses' advertisement.

6   Window glass fixed direct to framing.

7   Only one half-drop window per side per saloon.

8   Variable opening ventilators to be fitted to both forward-facing windows at front of upper saloon and a similar ventilator to nearside front bulkhead window.

9   Seats to be upholstered in leather or other suitable material.

10   Interior mouldings, cappings, pillars, etc. to be finished in natural grain; ceilings in enamel or cellulose.

11   Exterior to be given one coat of approved primer; the two further coats of approved paint.

12   Regulation white edging to be applied.

13   Rear registration to be painted on offside vestibule glass.

14   An aperture large enough to accommodate any standard type of destination indicator to be provided in upper saloon front panelling. No rear or side indicators to be fitted.

The first body to this austerity design was fitted to an 'unfrozen' Leyland TD7 chassis in late 1941 and was followed by many more as the war progressed.

It had been intended that the 'matching' chassis be built by both Leyland and Guy and 500 were ordered from each manufacturer in 1941. The Guys were delivered

The lower deck interior of a 'utility' bus showing wooden slatted seats and limited interior lighting. (*OS*)

The upper deck facing forward – note single skin ceiling. (*OS*)

And an upper deck rear-facing view. (*OS*)

between September 1942 and mid-1943 but Leyland had, in the meantime, been instructed to cease all civilian production and hence were unable to fulfil their contract. It was not obvious how to make good the shortfall but fortunately Daimler was able to recommence production from December 1942 (having been bombed out of its Coventry factory) and was able to supply 100 of its CWG5 model in early 1943, followed by 600 of the CWA6 from later the same year.

Once the few 'unfrozen' examples had been allocated there were no more full-sized single-deck vehicles produced until 1944. Their place was taken by the Bedford OWB, a basic bus, specifically designed to use the minimum of essential resources. Over 3,300 were built, although not all saw PSV use; many were used by government departments and some were exported. They became a common sight throughout Britain.

Aspects of the Production and Allocation Process
Strict conditions had to be met by operators in order to obtain new vehicles. They had to already be in possession of 'a permit to acquire a new vehicle'; then complete form VC1(P); stating whether high-bridge or low-bridge model was required, indicate a preferred bodybuilder and submit the request to the local RTC. There was no guarantee that the specification would be met but, in theory, it was permissible to exchange vehicles after delivery. Total requirements were then submitted to the MoWT, accompanied by the RTC's comments as to who should be given priority. A quota

An official view of the standard wartime single-deck bus. This was one of the first Bedford OWBs with Duple bodywork (EDG 392) and was supplied to Roy Grindle & Sons, Cindleford, in July 1942.

Oxford bus station during the war, with obligatory OWB, a Newbury Leyland Lion and an ST, on loan to City of Oxford from London Transport. (*OS/DHDS*)

was issued to each RTC who was responsible for the final allocation to individual operators. The allocation had to be taken up within a month and the order placed with the bodybuilder otherwise it was forfeit.

A few general comments indicated a certain amount of dissatisfaction with this procedure. The Public Service Transport Association had its 'knuckles rapped' by MoWT for suggesting chassis modifications directly to Guy, and was reminded that any alterations require prior approval of MoS, but the PSTA's main complaint was that it had not been not consulted re 'Utility Bus' specification. There was further concern that individual operators were trying to negotiate modifications to standard utility bodywork directly with the builders. This was also prohibited.

Other comments include the following:

Derby Corporation refused Pickering bodywork.
Eastern National refused their allocation of ten vehicles (no reason given).
London Transport needs 360 vehicles – 'not fussy as to specification'.
Area 6 (Southern) were offered twenty-two vehicles but sixteen were not taken up.
Area 8 (South Wales) asked for forty-one but only thirty-two accepted as most operators wanted a six-cylinder version (which was in short supply).

The bodies were built principally by Duple, Park Royal, Brush and Roe with lesser numbers provided by Pickering, Strachans, Massey, Weymann, Northern Counties and Northern Coach Builders. Although all were supposed to be to the same design, each bodybuilder had their own distinctive feature making identification of the manufacturer an easy matter. Further regulation required all deliveries after March 1943 to have wooden seats but from 1945, as restrictions eased, so did the specification, with later examples incorporating more 'domed panelling, upholstered seats, safety glass and additional opening windows'. These refinements were introduced as soon as individual bodybuilding schedules permitted.

An exceptional case was that of East Lancashire Coachbuilders whose wartime bodies were to 'peacetime' specification. Early in the war, part-built bodies (for Barrow and others) were transferred from English Electric to them for completion. Only Leyland chassis were dealt with, receiving bodies either to high-bridge specification, using their own standard parts, or low-bridge utilising Leyland bodyframes. Other work included re-bodies and repairs.

As scarce resources were allocated to double-deckers, new single-deck production was restricted to 1,300 Bedford OWB lightweight models, although, as with double-deckers, there was significant re-bodying of older heavyweight chassis. The OWB had a standard body, in the majority of cases by Duple, but some by Roe, SMT or Mulliner. Unlike the double-deck body, it was often difficult to easily identify the bodybuilder.

Lack of materials and other circumstances meant that wartime production never reached the target set by the MoS, which, in itself, was considerably below the estimate (over 20,000) of new vehicles actually needed. Total double-deck production, by the end of 1944, eventually materialised as 700 Daimlers (100 CWG5s and 600 CWA6s), 2,000 Guys and 110 trolleybuses.

AEC trolleybus (KY 8208) was Bradford Corporation number 605, and was delivered in 1934 with an English Electric body. This was replaced in 1944 by this utility example by Brush. (*OS*)

Utility buses under construction at the Brush works. (*OS*)

Midland Red, Guy Arab 2558 (HHA 10) with its Weymann utility body was allocated to the company in 1944. Many of these vehicles were rebuilt and modernised after the war. (*OS/CFK*)

The conductress is in the process of changing the destination on Midland Red Weymann bodied, 'utility' 2559 (HHA11). (*OS/CFK*)

Birmingham Corporation Duple-bodied utility Daimler (FOP 338) shows all the signs of hard wartime work despite being new in 1943. (*OS/CFK*)

Crosville utility Guy (FFM) 218 was new with this NCME body in 1942. Note 'Air Raid Shelter' sign by the bus stop somewhere between Crewe and Chester. (*OS/CFK*)

An example of the ubiquitous Bedford OWB: GKN 420 was delivered to Newman, Hythe, Kent, in 1943. (*OS/DHDS*)

Some interesting vehicles in this 1943 wartime line-up including: Duple-bodied OWB (CMO 624) and Thorneycroft (EKP 140). (*OS/DHDS*)

CNJ 887 is a typical Duple-bodied OWB. This one is operated by Mrs J. Sergeant of East Grinstead from whence, it is seen, en route to Cowden. (*OS/DHDS*)

A study in Bedford OWB rear ends as operated by Norfolk independents. EVF 4 and FAH 621 have Duple bodies whist EPW 650 and 833 are Mulliner. This is a post-war photograph as all have upholstered seats but those in FAH 621 are in 'perimeter' configuration. The location is King's Lynn. (*OS/CFK*)

Other Options

This severely restricted supply meant other methods of creating capacity had to be considered. A programme of adopting perimeter seating was already proving relatively successful. Authority was also given for the one-man operation of any single-deck vehicle subject to the approval of the local RTC. By 1943 the capacity problem was taxing 'government minds' resulting in a formal review of possible solutions. These embraced an articulated bus, of which four were already in use (in Liverpool and Mansfield), conversion of single-deckers to double-deckers, a trailer bus (as used in many European countries) and an intriguingly named 'stand-sit bus'.

Perimeter Seating

In September 1941 a new Standing Passengers Order was announced. This empowered the RTC to authorise the carriage, in single-deckers, of a number of standing passengers equivalent to the number of seats provided, but not exceeding a maximum of thirty such passengers. This was enacted on a case-by-case basis requiring inspection of all vehicles concerned by a certifying officer to ensure they had adequate grab rails or straps. Such operation was restricted to routes approved by both the RTC and the local trade union representative.

Crosville were the most enthusiastic company in adopting perimeter seating, as seen in this example.

The Ministry was very keen to introduce this additional capacity and demanded regular progress reports from each Traffic Area. The first one (dated September 1941) showed that some operators responded quite quickly, whist others were less enthusiastic:

North Midland (24/9/41) – 23 under conversion: Trent (4); Chesterfield (3); United Counties (10); Lincolnshire Road Car (6).

Southern The following stated they will not do any conversions: Aldershot (routes too long); Bournemouth (very few s/d vehicles); Bere Regis and King Alfred (no factory traffic), whilst Southdown and Thames Valley expressed their intention to convert some vehicles and other operators stated they now allowed standing on coaches.

SW Region – operators have safety concerns relating to tyres and propose no conversions.

NE Region – report of United Auto conversions for routes from Richmond to Catterick Camp .

NW Region – approvals as follows:

Ribble 28 SHMD+ 20
NWRCC* 87 Preston 6
Crosville 101 Manchester 5
Ashton 2 Magnet 1
Rochdale 4 Chester 15
Lancaster 16
*North Western Road Car Company.
+ Stalybridge, Hyde, Mossley & Duckinfield Joint Transport.

Action was not as speedy as the government would have liked, hence in December 1941 a memo from the Minister was sent to all RTCs expressing concern about lack of progress with conversions and 'wishes to be assured that the greatest possible effort is being made to secure fullest use of available vehicles'. Operators responded that they did not see perimeter seating as a workable solution to the capacity problem with Midland Red in particular, explaining why its vehicles were unsuitable for adaptation. Obtaining approval from the TGWU was also proving problematical. By the following summer, the further lack of progress led to the Minister reminding operators that he had compulsory powers to make them comply but 'he had not yet chosen to use them'. This prompted a further flurry of 'excuses' including a letter from RTC (Northern) making a case against mixed sexes travelling on converted vehicles due to the close proximity of passengers. However, it was noted that NE and N Wales were more pro-active than other areas, due mainly to the Crosville company. In Scotland, Alexander had tried the alternative of removing all seats in rear of vehicle, which had proved more acceptable to passengers.

The Minister never used his compulsory powers nor was there ever any serious attempt to go against the will of unions in this matter thus, in the end the scheme was deemed a 'partial success'. Statistics continued to be compiled on a regular basis until the end of the war but the process was effectively complete by mid-1943.

Two further examples of perimeter seating.

Summary Progress (All Areas)

31 March 1942: 1,026   15 November 1943: 2,061
31 July 1942: 1,357   15 December 1943: 2,068
15 April 1943: 2,040   15 May 1944: 2,128
15 July 1943: 2,102   15 September 1945: 2,116

Single-Deck to Double-Deck Conversions

Another approach to increasing overall capacity, in the absence of an adequate supply of double-deck vehicles, was to convert single-deck vehicles to double-deck. It was noted that, prior to 1943, Walter Alexander had already converted 100 Leyland Tiger TS7 models to Titan TD4 specification with the assistance of Leyland Motors. The task entailed: replacement of chassis side members, new propeller shafts, new springs and new tyres. The Government adopted this project, producing a plan to convert 250 TS7 chassis to TD4 specification. This involved Leyland supplying chassis frames (drilled for TD4) to MoS, chassis modifications, and removal of existing body, to be done by operators. New d/ds were to be built at rate of five per week by each of MoS-nominated bodybuilders (Alexander, Beadle, Burlingham, East Lancs and Northern Coach Builders). The programme was to be organised by MoWT who would prepare a 'technical note' on how to effect conversion and the bus industry Operators' Committee would be invited to nominate participating companies.

The operators' formal response to this proposal was first to challenge the need for so many conversions. They were not happy to utilise 'relatively new' TS7s, pointing out that there would be additional demand on their already-stretched maintenance facilities and they would prefer the 'nominated' bodybuilders to undertake major repairs on existing vehicles. Secondly, they queried the cost relative to the additional capacity achieved as this was about six passengers per vehicle after allowing for the elimination of standees on single-deckers.

The Government was not impressed by this counter-argument and instructed that 'conversions should be carried out a.s.a.p and resistance from operators overcome'. Accordingly the RTC set about identifying suitable vehicles for conversion but the only significant offer was 100 in the West Midlands Area. Other traffic areas were unable to find any takers (Trent had already converted fifteen Daimlers and Gosport one AEC); hence, with insufficient numbers the proposal was officially cancelled in March 1944 with the instruction that 'the released body building capacity be re-allocated'. Alexander continued with the scheme converting a further 104 vehicles by the end of the war for use by Scottish operators.

Articulated Buses

Another of the schemes to increase capacity in the industry was the articulated bus. Two separate attempts were made; one in 1941/2 and another in 1943/4 but neither made any significant contribution.

During 1941 the Government authorised the production of four examples, the first being completed in August. In the meantime operators were canvassed as to their views on operating such vehicles. Their response states that 'articulated buses cannot be regarded as a substitute for double-deckers' for the following reasons: they are longer than existing vehicles and could foul other traffic at turns; they had a higher risk of overturning as large number of passengers will affect stability; they are difficult to reverse; the driver is unable to see entrances and the conductor has great difficulty moving round inside. In conclusion they did not recommend they be introduced.

At the Regional Traffic Commissioners' Conference in March 1942 it was stated that four vehicles had been constructed. Two (for Liverpool Corporation) had Bedford OXC tractor units and were built by Dyson/Roe. Total capacity was sixty-five (thirty-eight seats plus twenty-seven standing) with registrations GKA 287/8. The others (for Mansfield & District) had Commer motive power and bodywork by British Trailer Corporation/Weymann and a capacity of thirty-eight. They were to be registered FVO 762/3.

Because the design did not meet Construction & Use Regulations (by virtue of their articulation) they were granted a 'Special Types Authorisation', which permitted use in public service 'for experimental purposes only'. This became effective on 3 June 1942 after which the Mansfield examples took up normal service duties and the Liverpool ones operated exclusively on a works service from Black Bull to Kirkby. The speed limitation of 20 mph gave difficulties in maintaining the timetable in Mansfield but no such problem arose in Liverpool.

One of two Commer articulated buses which were operated on an experimental basis in Mansfield. (*OS/CFK*)

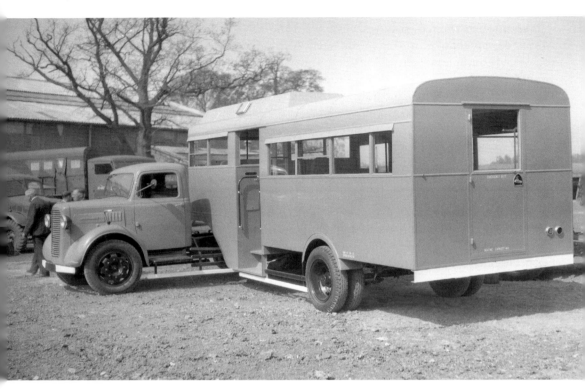

Another view of one of the pair of articulated Commer buses. (*OS/CFK*)

Interior of the Mansfield articulated buses.

Liverpool continued to use theirs until 1944 after which they were converted to mobile canteens remaining in use until the 1960s. It is not known how long the Mansfield examples continued in use but they passed to Notts & Derby Electricity Supply Company (a sister Balfour Beatty Company) in 1944 and remained with its successor (East Midlands Electricity Board) until the early 1960s.

Although many similar buses were built for internal use at Royal Ordnance Factories and other industrial sites, no further examples appeared in public service. However, in 1943, Sir Geoffrey Burton (director general of mechanical equipment in the Ministry of Supply) suggested that single-deck chassis should be modified as tractor units for articulated buses, Such was his enthusiasm (and influence) that a prototype was produced based on an ex-WD unit which was said to be the equivalent of an AEC Regal. The bodywork was a joint British Trailers/MCW product with fifty-four seats, two nearside doors and one offside emergency exit.

Called the 'Utility Trailer Bus' it was demonstrated to operators, unions and MoWT on 17 February 1944 and met with the response that it was 'a resurrection of an idea of 2–3 years ago and its shortcomings were the same as those identified at the time'. The Government stated that it 'would prefer the resources to be used in fitting utility bodies to ex-War Office chassis' and nothing more was heard of this second incarnation.

Other Permutations

Trailer Bus

This idea was initiated by Sir Leonard Franklin OBE in a letter to the Minister of War Transport, possibly after experiencing the concept in Lucerne. Having been asked for their comments, London Transport stated that they were slower than current buses, would be difficult to negotiate on corners, and it had concerns about braking procedures. There were few suitable routes and queuing would also pose a problem as would the need for an extra conductress.

There is a note on file to say that Barton presented a similar idea to the MoWT in 1941 and was told to 'develop the articulated bus or convert single-deckers to double'. A similar approach from Gosport & Fareham two years later was referred to the local RTC.

Stand-Sit Omnibus

Identification of this vehicle has proved difficult. The only reference is a note in a file at Kew (dated 9 August 1943) which states 'prototype constructed & inspected but general view is that it was not viable as only provides an additional six seats'.

The 'hunt for 1,000 buses on the Isle of Man'

At a meeting of Merseyside Industrial Traffic Consultation Committee on 19 August 1941 it was suggested that up to 1,000 buses were lying unused on the Isle of Man. A

A Bedford articulated bus at the Roe factory. This is possibly one of the two examples run experimentally in Liverpool from June 1942.

The 'second' attempt at an articulated bus used a shortened AEC chassis as motive power. It was even less successful than the previous design as none entered PSV service.

The 'less than appealing' interior of the AEC articulated vehicle.

Above: The twenty-three-strong batch of Southdown open-top Leyland TD1s (801–23) were progressively taken out of store during 1942 and fitted with temporary canvas top covers to enable them to be used in regular service. Here is 807 (UF 4807) posing alongside the coastal 'barbed-wire defences'. (*OS/CFK*)

Left: A rear view of Southdown 807. (*OS/CFK*)

Southdown manufactured 'home-made' roofs to enable their open-top vehicles to be used all year. Here is an example on a Leyland Titan (UF 4815) in Emsworth. (*OS/DHDS*)

letter was sent by MoWT to the Isle of Man Government seeking clarification but in the meantime the numbers had changed; either to 2,000 (per a note from the NWRTC on 23 September) or 1,000 seats (comprising fifty twenty-seat charabancs)! The official reply stated that 'the only surplus vehicles on the island were twenty and ten respectively, in the fleets of Isle of Man Road Services and Douglas Corporation, plus an unspecified number of charabancs with small operators'. (*Source: MT55/368*)

9

Alternative Fuels

Producer Gas

Operators were encouraged to find alternative propulsion methods in order to reduce the demand for petrol and diesel; the main substitute was producer gas, as a great deal of development work had already been undertaken by a number of independent companies. This principle required each vehicle to tow a trailer in which the gas was produced. Solid fuel (preferably anthracite) was loaded from sacks into the top of a hopper. After starting the bus engine on petrol (or diesel), a lighted coal-gas torch was inserted into the base of the hopper and the fuel ignited. The torch was removed and air drawn in through a vertical stack pipe to a water-cooled nozzle to produce a miniature blast furnace effect. The gas that came from the fire (a mixture of carbon monoxide, methane, hydrogen and steam) was filtered and purified and passed through an air-tight tube to the bus. Here it was mixed with air via a series of valves controlled by the driver to provide an effective substitute for petrol.

Initial experiments were begun as early as 1937 by AEC, who tested all the producer-gas systems then in use throughout Europe in examples of their chassis. Most required a trailer but with the French 'Bellay' system the gas-producing unit was carried on a rear extension to the chassis, giving obvious benefits to vehicle manoeuvrability. A separate British company – Gas Producers (Bellay) Ltd – was set up to develop the technology but only test running was permissible until Construction & Use regulations were amended in late 1939 to permit the greater weights and length required by the equipment.

The legislation had severely restricted development as any fitment to existing vehicles would necessitate a reduction in payload, which, combined with an approximate 33 per cent decrease in performance, made the whole exercise unattractive. Despite this a number of companies continued to experiment including complete buses constructed by Gilford and Sentinel. Glasgow Corporation also persevered with the, technically more difficult, conversion of diesel engine vehicle using one each of Bellay, Bristol, *Worldwin* and *BVP* equipment.

There were numerous types of producer gas trailer – two different makes are depicted here. (*OS/CFK*)

A new unit being inspected, probably by representatives of the trade press. (*OS/CFK*)

After the outbreak of war, operators were encouraged to convert a proportion of their fleets to run on producer gas but only London Transport and the Tilling Group showed any real enthusiasm. By May 1942, they had converted all the Eastern National buses at Maldon garage to run on producer gas, followed, in 1942, by the depots at Clacton and Cromer, the latter the responsibility of Eastern Counties. The equipment used was of ENOC design and constructed by the Bristol Tramways & Carriage Company Ltd (a subsidiary of Tilling).

Other operators were less enthusiastic so the MoWT issued a directive in October 1942 to all major bus operators requiring them to convert 10 per cent of their fleet to run on producer gas by July 1943. As part of this initiative the government ordered 3,000 trailers and associated parts from Bristol and a further 1,000 from Wylie Harris & Co. (formerly HSG) and offered training and expertise in their use. Arrangements were made for foreman mechanics of fifty-seven bus companies to attend a course at one of the three Tilling depots, which only operated PG vehicles. Other advice offered was to only select flat routes, to ensure adequate turning facilities and to amend timetables to reduce lay-overs to a minimum, as the gas units were less efficient when subject to prolonged stationary periods.

Nevertheless the effort required to run such vehicles was still considerable – there was a need for specific technical expertise to convert vehicles with the subsequent maintenance of both bus and trailer. While Government help was available in the form of technical assistance, no financial incentives were offered. The performance of producer-gas vehicles

Eastern National EV 1305 appears to have just returned to Maldon garage. It is on trade plates, in wartime grey livery and equipped with a PG trailer. (*OS/CFK*)

Eastern Counties converted their entire allocation at Cromer depot to producer gas. Here, two female staff refuel a unit. (*OM/CFK*)

Eastern Counties CFV 860 complete with gas trailer. (*OS/CFK*)

A particularly fine picture of Eastern Counties CVF 858 with PG trailer at Cromer Bus Station. (*OS/CFK*)

Above and below: Eastern National PG buses at Maldon bus station. (*OS/CFK*)

Additional facilities, including coal storage, were required to support PG operations. (*OS/CFK*)

The additional gas tank as fitted to an Eastern National vehicle. (*OS/CFK*)

Next three pages: Hicks Bros of Braintree was an enthusiastic user of producer gas to power its vehicles, as depicted in this series of pictures, presumably taken as part of a demonstration to the trade press. (*OS/CFK*)

was greatly inferior to their petrol counterparts, thus timekeeping was compromised and they were totally unsuitable for hilly routes. Further problems were the need for regular stops to attend to the burner and difficulties in reversing at termini.

As stated above, the Tilling Group was reasonably enthusiastic with 107 recorded conversions and a plan for a maximum of 758: Bristol Omnibus Company (111); Crosville (101); United (87); Eastern Counties (81); United Counties (26); Thames valley (24); Cumberland (18); Brighton & Hove (11); Western National (60); Eastern National (57); West Yorkshire (45); Southern National (34), Hants & Dorset (33); Lincolnshire (25); Wilts & Dorset (22); Caledonian (14); Southern Vectis (9).

It is unlikely that any of these targets were achieved.

The next most prolific user was Midland Red who planned 140 conversions but, partly due to the design of the BMMO engine, only managed about thirty although the entire complement of Evesham garage was gas propelled. East Kent was also seen to be more enthusiastic than the average and South Wales Transport Company, being dissatisfied with 'proprietary' equipment, designed its own gas plant (known as the Ravenhill)

This and next page: Eastern National experimented with incorporating the PG unit within the body of the bus. Bristol HHT 459 was the selected vehicle as shown in this series of pictures. (*OS/CFK*)

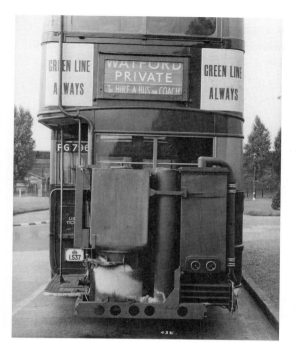 

Above left: An LT vehicle fitted with experimental PG unit on a rear extension as distinct to a separate trailer.

Above right: This experimental producer gas unit was built onto the bodywork of a Glasgow Corporation vehicle. (*OS*)

London Transport converted about 170 ST type double-deckers and nine Country Area T single-deckers to allow PG operation although some of them probably were not used in this mode (this is covered in detail in Tony Newman's book.). Again, the small number of such vehicles, compared to the total fleet size, indicated their unpopularity.

Further 'threats' from the Government did nothing to speed up the process of conversion, although most major operators ran a few 'token' examples. Walsall Corporation managed two for a six-month period in 1943; Ribble converted eleven; Lincolnshire Road Car had ten trailer units but there is no record of these being used and even Eastern National failed to reach the 10 per cent target. With the general improvement in fuel supplies the scheme was officially terminated in September 1944 and most operation ceased immediately but some Tilling companies persevered. Brighton & Hove stopped in December 1944 as did Eastern Counties, United Automobile and West Yorkshire, but two vehicles were still in use in Bristol the following April and the final conversion back to petrol was by East Midland in February 1946.

Although not part of a conventional bus network, possibly the largest fleet of such vehicles was employed to transport construction workers to the massive explosives factory which became ROF Swynnerton in Staffordshire. The main contractor, Sir Alexander Gibb, purchased forty-four Leyland LT2 Lions that had been sold by Ribble in early 1940. These passed via Wintour, a London dealer, to Ennis Sentinel Ltd who adapted them to run on producer gas using their proprietary equipment. Records confirm that they were purchased by the contractor (Sir Alexander Gibb) as an agent of MoS. Responsibility for operation was delegated to Potteries Motor Traction who appeared to use an open-air site rather than one of their depots. Additionally there were at least six further vehicles (another ex-Ribble Lion and five Albions) but it is not known if these were also powered by PG. Once the construction phase of the project was finished the vehicles reverted to petrol and passed to new owners.

Left: An ex-Ribble Tiger, one of several used to carry construction workers to ROF Swynnerton, operated on producer gas. (*Bus & Coach*)

Below: Part of the North Western producer-gas-powered fleet. This comprised pre-war Leyland TS4 and TS6 models fitted with utility Burlingham bodies in 1943. They reverted to petrol in 1946. (*Bus & Coach*)

There was competition to develop an effective gas producer for buses in the early part of the war. This advertisement relates to an 'Enness' experimental run from Southport to Rhyl in 1940.

Producer-gas vehicles in operation: 1 – Southern National 2979. Note that the town name has been deleted from the gas showroom to prevent identification of the location of the picture. (*OS/CFK*)

Producer-gas vehicles in operation: 2 – Royal Blue ATT 929. (*OS/CFK*)

Producer-gas vehicles in operation: 3 – Southern National DR 5198 amid a 'bleak wartime' landscape. (*OS/CFK*)

Producer-gas vehicles in operation: 4 – Crosville Leyland TS2 173 (FM 5220) had its original 1929 Leyland body replaced by this ECW example in 1936. This view was taken in Wrexham; alongside is one of their ubiquitous Titans. (*OS/CFK*)

Producer-gas vehicles in operation: 5 – A front view of WNOC Dennis 615 (BTA 75) operating on producer gas. (*OS/JFP*)

A rare photograph of a Southdown bus powered by producer gas. (*E. Surfleet*)

Town Gas

Despite the government's preference for producer gas, some operators reinvented the system used during the First World War and propelled vehicles with town gas (mixed with 10 per cent of fuel oil) carried in large bags installed on the roof of single-deckers, although there is a suggestion that someone went one further and filled an entire upper deck with the gas bag! Glasgow, Manchester, Burnley, Barton, South Shields and Yorkshire Woollen were known to have adopted this method for a short while, although the total number of conversions was probably less than ten.

Alternatively a liquid fuel could be produced from town gas; this was favoured by South Shields and Wallasey Corporations and the latter became 100 per cent reliant on this method by August 1942.

Bus & Coach for December 1941 highlights Taylor of Chester who converted at least two of his coaches to run on compressed (coal) gas. It is not known to what extent his example was followed among private operators.

Creosote

A number of operators were reported in the trade press as experimenting with running buses on a creosote mixture. Among these were Rochdale, Halifax and Southport corporations but only Southport persevered, reportedly exceeding a million miles by March 1942.

Barton repeated their First World War experiments and equipped this Leyland with a roof-mounted bag containing town gas. (*OS/ CFK*)

Another view of Barton ARR 183. (*OM/CFK*)

South Shields fitted this framework to Daimler 107 (CU 3205) to hold a bag of town gas. (*R. C. Davis*)

Above: South
Shields 107
(CU 3205) seen
in operation
complete with
gas bag.

Right: A
Manchester
Crossley
adapted to run
on town gas.

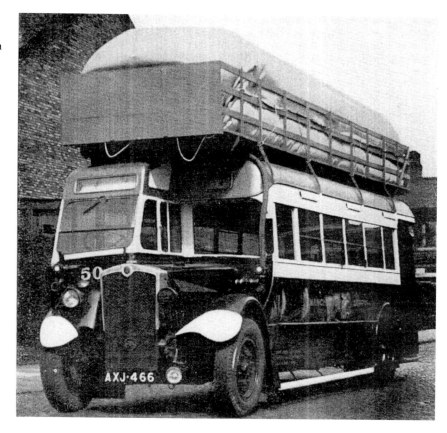

Learning from the past? Midland Red buses powered by town gas during the First World War. (*OS*)

Other Systems

Petro (a USA high-octane fuel) was used for a time by Walsall Corporation (and possibly others) but it seriously damaged petrol engines, and so it was soon discontinued. Northern General experimented with 'compressed gas' in 1939 but did not continue.

10

Making Do with Limited Resources

Suggestions for Increased Operational Efficiency

By November 1941 capacity constraints were so severe that they were affecting the ability of essential war workers to reach the factories. In addition to measures to improve the capacity of vehicles, the government sought operating efficiencies. This was to be achieved by removing the previous 'boundary' restrictions and protected fares but also a more radical review was undertaken as it was perceived there would be benefits through greater coordination and possible merging of organisations that operated in the same area to 'improve economies of scale' and streamline the provision of fixed facilities and maintenance. Amalgamation would also reduce the number of spare vehicles required but the main benefit would be that the RTC could achieve easier coordination of transport in his area. Each RTC was charged with evaluating the possibilities, resulting in an interim report, which acknowledged that there would be severe resistance from councils who saw their bus fleet as a symbol of local pride. There was also an appreciation that one solution would not suit all areas and that some would be more successful than others.

Mr Stirk (the Nottingham RTC) was one of the former. He reported that empty seats on all buses into Nottingham were now available to all (i.e. no longer any restriction on use of Trent but fares were *double* those on Corporation buses), the practice of imposing transfers onto Nottingham Corporation vehicles (for works destinations within the municipal area) had now been discontinued with private operators permitted to undertake through journeys, Corporation vehicles were now operating up to 20 miles beyond the municipal boundary to munitions works and small operators had been grouped into a 'group lenders' scheme thus producing economies for all.

He also gave an opinion on the possibility of amalgamation of municipal operators in his area:

Cleethorpes was not regarded as economically viable and a merger with Grimsby was suggested.

Derby, on the other hand, was very efficient and no benefit would be gained from an amalgamation (with Trent). Protective fares had been waived for the duration of the war.

Grimsby was viable but no scope for joint operation except with Cleethorpes.

Lincoln was seen as too small to be efficient but the Labour council were not prepared to talk to the Lincolnshire Road Car Company.

Leicester was efficient and had good relations with Midland Red.

Northampton was financially 'precarious' and would benefit from amalgamation with United Counties Omnibus Company.

West Bridgford already has a joint service with Nottingham.

In the North West, the Regional Traffic Commissioner directed that Preston-based Ribble and Scout 'streamline' their operations in order to save fuel, rubber and other scarce resources. Accordingly, on 16 September 1939 they introduced a coordinated service between Preston and Blackpool which led, ultimately (from 19 December 1941), to one of the most far-reaching schemes ever introduced in the industry. All receipts were pooled, each company receiving a fixed percentage (Ribble 60 per cent, Scout 40 per cent) in exchange for operating mileage in the same proportion. Scout conductors used Ribble tickets and machines and cashed in at Ribble offices. Additionally (and

It was suggested that Grimsby Corporation be merged with neighbouring Cleethorpes to save costs but this was not pursued. However, this photograph shows how the name above the depot has been covered up to 'confuse' any potential enemy.

for an extra fee) Ribble performed all administrative work, licensing and publicity and also provided conductors to Scout for 'fill-in duties'. Scout was thus relieved of much administration.

Meanwhile, others were less successful. Empty seats on Green Line services between Tonbridge and Tunbridge Wells could not be made available 'for legal reasons' and a discussion occurred as to whether the RTC had the powers to direct Bournemouth Corporation to operate in Poole against the wishes of Poole Corporation. The decision was that the RTC could make this instruction provided he used his powers 'reasonably'.

Generally, though, RTCs were unsure of the extent of their powers in achieving coordination and sought support from the Government in this respect. This was not forthcoming as the Minister's advice was limited to merely urging the RTCs to use their best endeavours. However, the Northern RTC arranged a scheme for pooling works services in the Bishop Auckland area resulting in under-employed vehicles being released.

The paper continued with examples of successful cooperation between operators (Keighley, York, Bristol and Brighton). Lesser schemes were also noted in Gloucester, Worcester and Scarborough. All joint-working agreements were recorded by the Ministry who continued to update the information throughout 1942, 1943 and

A wartime view of a Southdown-Beadle-bodied Leyland TD4 in Tunbridge Wells. (*OS/DHDS*)

A typical wartime view of a United Counties Bristol (VV 8252). (*OS/CFK*)

1944. The following extract (by RTC), from a file at Kew, indicates the extent of such operations:

> **Midland**: noted operating agreements between Midland Red and the Corporations of Birmingham; West Bromwich; Coventry; Walsall.
> **NW Region**: had fourteen co-ordination agreements –thirteen between Ribble and (numerous) other operators and one between Crosville and Liverpool Corporation.
> **Southern**: noted the following – Hants & Dorset and Poole/Bournemouth; Southdown and Portsmouth; Thames Valley and Reading.
> **South Eastern**: Brighton Corporation and Southdown & Brighton Hove & District.
> **South West**: Bristol Tramways and Gloucester Corporation; Bristol Corporation. Plymouth Corporation and Western National.
> **North East**: Huddersfield Corporation and Hansons.

Although these continued to be recorded they generated no further action, nor were any of the other ideas pursued.

11

Personnel Matters

Staff Shortages

Lack of personnel was the most severe problem facing the industry throughout the war.

Many maintenance staff and drivers were in the reserve forces and left immediately war was declared in September 1939. Drivers were replaced by the 'promotion' of conductors and they, in turn, by the recruitment of conductresses. It was not as easy to replace the skilled maintenance workers and although some women were employed in the workshops, they did not have the relevant skills and were therefore restricted to lesser tasks such as fuelling and cleaning. The very few skilled women who were available were attracted to the new government factories where conditions and pay were better. There was also a gradual drift of drivers to these new establishments where alternative jobs were often more appealing than bus work in the blackout.

The general upheaval of the first few months of the war with staff losses, fuel rationing, changes in demand for services, requisitioning of vehicles and premises, etc. made it very difficult for the affected bus companies to organise their resources. Some (especially seaside operators) had surplus vehicles while others (with new government factories and large numbers of inbound refugees) were short.

Walsall Corporation provided services to new factories by hiring coaches and drivers from Blackpool and Morecambe corporations; the drivers lived in the Midlands and often worked at the factory as well. This arrangement lasted from 1942 to 1945. The need for conductors on Birmingham Corporation and Midland Red works services was met by using regular travellers to perform these duties on a voluntary basis.

In October 1943 the MoWT held a conference which included representatives of English and Scottish operators, union representatives and MoL officials to discuss the shortage of labour in the industry. Concerns had been raised at the industry's general inability to retain sufficient staff to provide an adequate service. It was reported that 118 out of 130 passenger transport undertakings were experiencing labour shortages but all municipal services (except Glasgow) were still managing to cope. 'Wastage' was

Buses were used in many support roles, like this Wallasey Corporation Leyland PLSC converted to a kitchen for civil defence personnel.

exceeding 'recruitment' as staff were leaving due to misconduct (20 per cent), domestic problems (19 per cent), health (50 per cent), training (4 per cent) and other reasons (7 per cent); there were unacceptable delays in the recruitment process. The result was that remaining staff were working 'excessive hours' necessitating a seven-day week for many. Complicating factors were identified, such as revised service patterns (as a consequence of Government Directives), which had created difficulties for some staff in travel to work, and producer-gas operations were more labour intensive than conventionally fuelled buses.

By this date, there were almost no additional women available to recruit and there was great reluctance from them to join the industry, as many employers had not updated welfare facilities to accommodate them (Ribble was particularly poor in this regard) as the following indicates:

The RTC is concerned at the high numbers of potential recruits rejected [of 180 applicants since July 1941 only 14 were employed] and the fact that no provision is made towards their expenses. The MoL [whose role is to fill vacancies] was [also] concerned about this and the company's inability to retain female staff – not least because of the poor facilities. Accordingly they arranged a meeting with Major Hickmott [General Manager] but he was unwilling to make any concessions to the increasing proportion of female staff. He is quoted as saying 'I founded the company and I am going to run it!' However he did agree to speak to the general manager of Crosville [who were considered better employers in this respect] on the matter.

The net result was that the RTC would no longer direct conductresses to work for Ribble nor would the MoL fill any vacancies.

Conductresses and Other Female Labour

Female labour was critical to the provision of wartime transport, its importance exemplified by Midland Red where the proportion of the labour force grew from 8 per cent to 40 per cent. A change of this magnitude was not without problems, some of which seemed unnecessary when viewed from a modern perspective. Traditionally women tended to work within a narrow range of jobs (domestic service, shop assistants, factories) but the war required them suddenly to become involved in many practices that, up to then, were 'male only', of which the bus industry was a classic example. Hence, there was a great deal of apprehension about what was regarded as a major cultural change. While some employers made the employment of women as easy as possible (e.g. Manchester and Birmingham corporations), others went to great lengths to put off the inevitable (Chester and Southampton preferring older men until there were insufficient to meet requirements). Even the more enlightened companies had problems of recruitment as the nature of the work (with its irregular hours, early starts, difficult customers, responsibility for cash, exposure to blackouts and air raids) did not appeal. The Ministry of Labour found it was unable to direct staff into the industry and the scheme for mobile conductresses who could transfer between operators to offset the greatest need was very unpopular with both individuals and employers (*Passenger Transport* from 14 January 1944 records the fact that fourteen girls refused to transfer from Newcastle to Birmingham). In a drastic attempt to maintain complements, women eligible for call-up were allowed to be conductresses instead and some were even transferred back from the military. Absenteeism and staff shortages dogged the industry until servicemen returned in 1945.

It was not just the culture issue that discouraged action; there were problems with conditions of employment. The unions did not want juniors (i.e. those under twenty) and demanded women be paid the equivalent male rate, work a standard forty-eight-hour week and have a contract for a specific time, even though the latter was impossible to determine given the unknown wartime needs. This was too restrictive for the employers and it was not until April 1940 that national terms were agreed (through the Ministry of Labour and the Industrial Court) wherein women were allowed to be paid slightly lower hourly rates and to have a shorter contractual week. The full findings of the Industrial Court were that women conductors should be eighteen or over; for the first six months they should receive not less than 90 per cent of equivalent male pay rate, thereafter their pay would be at the equivalent to men, except for those under twenty-one who would remain on the 90 per cent rate until attaining that age. Conditions of employment were identical to men save that the guaranteed week was forty hours (at the individual employer's discretion) compared with the male week of forty-eight hours with all additional hours worked to be paid as overtime. Contracts of employment were specifically for 'duration of war' only. These new terms became applicable from 19 April 1940.

The novelty of women in the industry is reflected in the concern the trade press had for their uniforms. The issue of whether they should wear 'skirts or slacks' seems to have been debated in many council chambers and board rooms but it is probably indicative of the times that no women's views are reported. Facilities, both in the depots and at termini, were often primitive and acted against recruitment of women. However, women seem to have fared better with the smaller operators; Stratford Blue immediately employed women and they soon outnumbered the men, a situation which

green material with half belts, and the box-pleated skirt has red piping down each side. Green N.A.A.F.I. hats with a black band and red piping complete an attractive ensemble.

2

In London the conductorettes will be habited in a dark grey worsted material. The tunic will be single breasted, shaped, with a stitched-down belt all round and side pockets. It will be buttoned up to the neck. The skirt will be divided and a little more than knee length. For summer wear, the women will be issued with a dark grey dust coat, double breasted with double breasted lapels, shaped and with a belt at the back. The uniform will be piped with blue. The caps are of French kepi style of the same material as the uniform, with a 1½in. band of blue. The crown is piped with blue and a metal "London Transport" badge will be worn, white for central buses, green for country buses and red for trams.

3

What is called a divided skirt uniform has been decided on for the Leeds women conductors. The colour scheme is navy blue (the material is serge), with red piping.

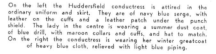

On the left the Huddersfield conductress is attired in the ordinary uniform and skirt. They are of navy blue serge, with leather on the cuffs and a leather patch under the punch shield. The lady in the centre is wearing a summer dust coat, of blue drill, with maroon collars and cuffs, and hat to match. On the right the conductress is wearing her winter greatcoat of heavy blue cloth, relieved with light blue piping.

A simple two-piece costume of unrelieved navy serge is favoured at Wolverhampton, the tunic single breasted with a belted back, and provided with chromium buttons. The skirt is quite plain, and the cap has a soft peak. The Wolverhampton girls are also issued with a navy gabardine raincoat, half belted, and with chromium buttons.

continued until the end of the war. Even in this country area there were less appealing aspects of the job. One lady recalls how airfield construction workers tormented her to such a degree that she struck out and injured one. The resulting investigation led to the services becoming 'contract' thus eliminating the necessity to collect fares.

ostume from of a jacket t pockets and and leather trousers are d have two rm is com- blouse and nd black ties, of cap with tops.

Manchester conductresses have single breasted indigo blue coats with four buttons. There are two pockets with flaps, and the sleeves have side slashes piped red on the cuff. The collar is also piped red. The plain skirt is worn 15ins. from the ground, and is also indigo blue. Cap is 3½in. deep with a soft crown which is covered in white cotton drill for summer wear. For winter use a single breasted overcoat is provided, of blue Melton, with piping as described for the jacket.

This smart Barrow uniform is o fine blue serge, piped with ligh blue, and with chromium plate buttons. The overcoat is of th same material, but one o heavier weight is provided fo winter use.

Opposite page: A selection of female uniforms.

Right: More female uniforms.

s are made up from o serge to the indi- the wearer—single tyle collar, pleated pockets with flaps, vent at the back. are made up to e material as the are made up of tunic and skirt, are with half belt and The collars are so they can be worn to the neck or turned weather conditions. lue, single breasted cuffs. Caps blue, igo serge with soft Gaiters of blue with zip fastener.

This Northern Coachbuilders utility body featured in the Trade Press as it was produced entirely by female labour.

Female drivers had been a feature of some rural routes for many years but the first double-decker drivers appeared in September 1941 at Luton, and were to become more common as the war progressed. By 1942 women were also working as inspectors at Southport; a particularly progressive undertaking that also employed female fitters by this date. Although relatively few, some women were to be found in a number of engineering departments, but their ultimate contribution to the industry was possibly the construction of an entire double-deck body by Northern Coach Builders using only female labour.

12

Increasing Ministry Involvement

A Selection of Vehicle Censuses

The Government was caught out during the early days of the war as it had no idea of the size of the country's bus fleets. Nor did it appreciate the additional demand created by the construction, and operation, of wartime airfields and factories which not only generated extra passengers, but also new locations, often distant from any town, thus significantly decreasing the efficiency of fleet utilisation. It had been assumed, with no basis to support the fact, that railways would carry most of the traffic and that there would be sufficient buses to meet other demands.

The official files contain a number of census returns from the war years: the first, in July 1940, comprises a breakdown of vehicle types by make/model/year of manufacture 'to assist with the provision of spare parts'. Within the total of 46,920 (analysed by manufacturer from ADC to Wolseley) there were some rather obscure marques including one each of Brockway, Citroën, Delage, Federal, Hudson and two each of Manchester and Nash.

The first attempt to quantify surplus capacity was a summary (by RTC) of out-of service buses in February 1941, which produced these totals:

Fit for service (unlicensed): s/d = 2,047; d/d = 119
Surplus to requirements: s/d = 685; d/d = 0
Available for transfer: s/d = 50

Lacking detail, this survey was found to be of little use; therefore, after the severe shortage of vehicles during 1941/2, the MoWT took the initiative in May 1942 to ascertain the 'true situation in regard to idle vehicles'. This new questionnaire was extremely comprehensive with four categories of return required for three separate classifications of vehicles. Vehicle types were analysed as s/d (below thirty-two seats); s/d (thirty-two seats or more) and d/d for which the following were required: licensed, maximum used in any one day, unlicensed and daily mileage by all licensed vehicles.

In addition details were sought re ambulance conversions and vehicles reserved for hospital evacuation, War Department, civil police and Queen's Messenger Service.

Other than generating correspondence within government departments and with the RTCs, no positive action is recorded as a consequence but it is possible that the information was used by RTCs for local purposes, and by Government in formulating plans for new vehicle construction. No written evidence survives to prove either of these suggestions.

United Automobile Services was one of a number of operators who protested that 'the questions did not give true position' and supplied supplemental answers clarifying that the following were all to be drawn from the licensed fleet:

Hospital evacuation: 35
War Department: 93
Civil police: 10
Queen's Messenger Service: 1

It also stated that UAS had ninety-three vehicles on hire from other operators employed by them as agents for A. M. Carmichael (contractors) re ROF Aycliffe. The vehicles were hired from the operators nearest the workforce's houses.

Legislation

The overall legislation within Emergency Powers (Defence) Road Vehicles (1939) had immediate major effects on the governance of road passenger transport operations in that it gave RTCs the power to requisition vehicles and other assets. The requirement to license staff, vehicles and routes was suspended and control exercised through a series of 'permits':

B – annual permit for driver or conductor of PSV.
C – vehicle permit (in lieu of PSV licence) – it was not necessary for a current Certificate of Fitness to qualify for such a permit.
D – related to modifications to a road service licence.
E – for a temporary route.
F – for a new 'permanent' service.

New services no longer required local authority consent, there was an increase in vehicle weights for new vehicles (to allow for use of heavier construction materials) and permitted standing passengers were increased from five to eight at all times. Also, detailed legislation was enacted to allow the operation of producer-gas vehicles.

As the war progressed, further legislation was introduced covering nearly every aspect of operations, including restrictions on hours, fuel, queue control, vehicle sale and purchase, fares and conductresses. (For full listing see Appendix 3.)

Trams also had masked headlights but were not affected by fuel restrictions or fare legislation. This is a Blackburn example seen in The Boulevard.

Fares and Services

Regulations were introduced prohibiting fare alterations without government approval. This resulted in a number of cases of detail being referred to the MoWT particularly in regard to workman's fares which had produced a number of anomalies as the extended working week now included staggered shifts and weekends. In 1940 an instruction was issued that all major operators were expected to charge workman's fares to eligible passengers, but small operators could ask for increases. The suggestion, by the operators, that discounted workman's fares were not required on Sunday (as workers were paid premium rates on this day) was not approved.

The matter was still proving contentious in April 1942 when a deputation from operators visited the MoWT to debate the workman's fares problem. One solution suggested was that operators sold bulk tickets to employers, as the Ribble company had successfully done. However, by this time there was increasing awareness of the growing profitability of operators as the war progressed; hence, the government was less impressed with operators' arguments of financial hardship.

In February 1940, principles were published against which the Government would grant fare increases. The emphasis was on applicant companies' financial situation and profitability and it required completion of an incredibly detailed submission to support their case. A problem arose with municipal companies as many made a contribution to the local rates and there was a view that this should be discontinued during the war. The background files (for use in adjudicating applications) include schedules detailing the 1939–40 financial position for many municipalities and private company dividends paid between 1930 and 1938. The intention was to use these as a benchmark against which to review the situation at the end of the war. The general view was that the issue was too complex to deal with centrally and individual applications were to be dealt with on their merits. Plymouth Corporation secured a general fare increase from 1 March 1940 under these arrangements. However, in June 1941 the Treasury stated that road passenger transport fares should be controlled so as not, in general, to rise further above the pre-war level than railway fares have risen (i.e. 16.66 per cent) but agreed 'certain elasticity should be used in applying the rule'. Applications soon diminished as increasing profitability meant that operators did not seek to raise fares after 1941.

A further directive, relating to fares, was issued in June 1941, with the principal objective of achieving fuel savings. Sunday mileage (except that exclusively for workmen) was to be reduced by 50 per cent; all fares which encouraged casual travel were to be discontinued; single fares (less than 2d) and returns (less than 4d) were to be withdrawn in areas where short-distant travel used excess resources; season tickets valued at less than 2s/9d per week, 10s/9d per month or 26s/9d per quarter should not be reissued and there was to be no duplication of services other than those already provided.

Transfers to Rail

To achieve the fundamental objective of encouraging the use of rail, rather than road, transport a number of specific fare revisions were approved to 'equalise' fares to discourage bus use. Known instances of this happening are Ulverston–Bowness, Newcastle–Scotswood Halt, and Oldham–Shaw.

A. H. Hardcastle

A. H. Hardcastle, a small operator based in Wold Newton near Driffield, has a specific file in The National Archive at Kew:

> It appears that Mr Hardcastle increased the fares on his Saturday-only service between Foxholes and Bridlington without the prior approval of the Regional Traffic Commissioner, in contravention of wartime legislation. The exact date of the increase is not stated but the 1944 file is in respect of a retrospective application and states that 'the increased fare has been operative for a year without any objection'.

The document comprises a Minute (dated 27 October 1944) from the North Eastern Regional Traffic Commissioner to the Routes & Charges Division of the MoWT together with an Income & Expenditure account and the reference to the fact that the twenty-seat bus used on the route also operates once a week from Wold Newton to Scarborough but has no other duties.

Despite the recommendation that the increased fare be approved, someone in the MoWT has taken the trouble to rework the Income & Expenditure (each totalling approximately £300) to prove that the small annual loss originally shown should be a profit of £2.

The file was returned to the RTC with the recommendation that 'he use his judgement as to whether the increase be approved'.

The vehicle was probably COP 939 Fordson BB18F with B20F body, new in February 1937 to Kiteley, Stockinford, and acquired by Hardcastle in February 1939. (*Source: PSV Circle*)

(*Source: MT56/269*)

13

Royal Ordnance Factories

Transport Needs of a Royal Ordnance Factory

By the end of the war, there was a total of forty-nine ROFs making bombs and ammunition. Some that had been in existence prior to the war saw increased activities but many were major establishments created on green field sites remote from existing urban areas. The larger ones such as Chorley, Aycliffe and Swynnerton employed thousands of staff who had to be transported daily. The policy was to use rail as the primary transport but this still left significant numbers to be carried by road. Buses were also required to transfer employees from the (usually specially constructed) station around the site and to and from the hostels provided. Unlicensed vehicles could be used on site and these often comprised a mixture of time-expired PSVs, articulated buses and other truck-based conveyances.

The scale and problems of providing transport to a new (unspecified) ROF factory were detailed in a TNA file: 'The factory was in an isolated location and had additional requirement for internal transport'.

In this example most of the emphasis was on rail transport but also mentions that the site included a number of hostels and that a considerable amount of 're-zoning' had taken place in that workers with homes nearest to the site had their employment transferred there. This action had saved 5,500 bus miles/week. A further 5,358 bus miles were saved through withdrawal of services that duplicated the railway and restricting the workforce's catchment area to a 30-mile radius.

At peak production the facility required a weekly service of 348 special trains plus 98 ordinary ones (presumably these include freight), 474 buses daily = 2,844/week, 810 daily journeys to hostels using factory-owned vehicles, plus an internal service fleet (50 seats + 15 standees) running 2,100 journeys/week. The factory owned 114 road vehicles including buses, canteen vans, cars, fire engines, etc. and operated special bus services to meet workers' trains. To simplify administration rail and bus tickets were distributed in pay packets at standard rates.

And the specific requirements of providing transport to the RAF site at Wombleton (North Riding) were noted in January 1943. The location and numbers of passengers

Former LT buses bought by Liverpool Corporation brought the majority of the former 'pirate' TD class from London Transport to serve new wartime factories. Eighty-four vehicles were acquired in total, although some were used for spare parts and did not enter service. Fleet number 63 (GO 1636) was a TD1 model with Dodson body new to Express in 1931 and latterly LT no. TD103.

More ex-London Transport TD class are seen in this view. Prominent is number 39 (KP 3055) a Short-bodied TD1, ex-TD146 and originally Maidstone & District. This was one of the few vehicles in green livery and displays the destination 'East Lancs Road' which is where many of the new government factories were located.

Wrexham ROF 'bus station' with Crosville vehicles borrowed from London Transport, Wallasey and others.

made it an unattractive proposition for operators and, even for those willing to provide vehicles, the RTC refused to grant extra fuel. Workers were told to use the train to Newton then travel by feeder bus for 2.5 miles. It was calculated that the 1,300-strong labour force, predominantly based in Scarborough, would have needed thirty-two individual buses using 5,000 gallons of fuel/month. As it happened fourteen vehicles were still required, which United Automobile Services were told to provide. They were reluctant to do so as they had no depot nearby and vehicles would be underutilised, so a solution was reached whereby MoL agreed to find fourteen drivers and United would use independent operators as much as possible; the drivers were employed by the contractors and did other work while on site. The source of all buses is not known but two United employees were stationed at the site for 'maintenance and engineering attendance (as required)'. Problems arose with reimbursement payments as Braithwaites (Stockton) had five vehicles on site and paid for eight hours/day (the staff also worked for a contractor), whereas United drivers were only paid four hours/ day. United also complained about the heavy wear on its vehicles, lack of cover at the site, no heaters (for bus radiators) and the fact that contract drivers abused the vehicles; hence, contract hire rates were considered inadequate and both United and Braithwaite announced their intentions to withdraw the service especially as the site contractor was a 'very slow payer'.

14

Wartime Publicity

Wartime publicity had a number of objectives: to remind people of the contribution the industry was making to the war effort, to encourage responsible use of the buses to enable essential workers to get to their employment unimpeded by shoppers and leisure travellers and to ensure the safe use of vehicles, particularly during the blackout.

An article in *Bus & Coach* (January 1943) detailed the Tilling Group's policy starting with an immediate campaign on the outbreak of war to control the number of rush hour passengers. Standardised, group-produced, advertisements were customised for local operators and displayed in provincial newspapers and on vehicles; the main themes being to discourage non-essential travellers and promote the staggering of office hours. Posters were also designed to complement other specific themes including: National Savings promotion campaigns, use of producer-gas vehicles, recruitment of women as conductresses, taking care during the blackout and abiding by 'queue regulations', as well as addressing special problems posed by Christmas and summer holidays.

In 1942, The Select Committee on National Expenditure indicated that the public were not aware of the problems facing the bus industry under wartime constraints and that transport employees did not feel directly involved in war work. They, therefore, suggested a comprehensive propaganda campaign as a result of which a series of four advertisements were commissioned. Titled 'Buses Go to Battle', they linked the bus industry to tanks and munitions workers, to the war factory and at the war factory. Again, customised to include the name of the local operator, they appeared in over 130 newspapers. To get a similar message to the wider public a series of similar posters were commissioned by the British Omnibus Companies Public Relations Committee entitled 'But for the Buses' emphasising the role of the bus in transporting vital war workers.

Manufacturers' advertisements in the trade press evolved as the war progressed, as indicated in *Bus & Coach*. Initially, apart from a significant reduction in quantity, there was little change in content but by April 1940 some began to make coded references, such as 'the present situation' or stating that 'deliveries could no longer be promised'. A more obvious indication of changing circumstances was an advert for Enness gas

MAY, 1944   BUS & COACH   Advertisements 25

THE ROAD TO RECONSTRUCTION

DUPLE Buses have earned a reputation during their journeys over millions of trouble-free miles. Sturdy coachwork that DUPLE built before the war is now performing yeoman service under arduous conditions. The modest utility designs differ only by the absence of sumptuousness. DUPLE Buses lead on every road. They will be foremost in reliability and comfort on the road to reconstruction.

DUPLE BODIES & MOTORS
LIMITED

EDGWARE ROAD, THE HYDE, HENDON, LONDON, N.W.9

Phone : COLINDALE 6412 (Pvt. Ex.)   Grams : "DUPLE, HYDE, HENDON"
Cables : "DUPLE, HENDON, LONDON"   Codes : BENTLEY'S, A.B.C. (5th Edtn.)

A Duple advertisement from May 1944.

A complete OWB could be yours for £825 provided you had the necessary permits. (*Bus & Coach*)

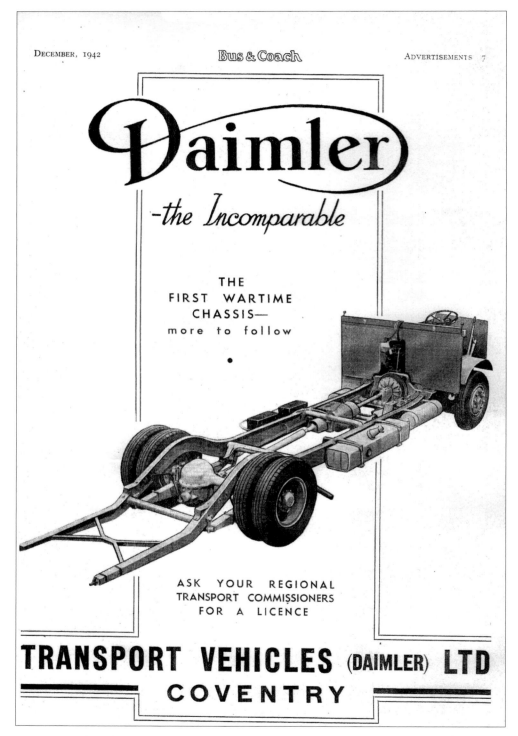

A 1942 Daimler advertisement following the company's re-establishment in Wolverhampton.

Travel only when you must

Leisure is necessary in wartime, but there's a limit to the decency of joy-riding. Remember, please, that the bus Companies in addition to their normal task of carrying the public, are conveying millions to and from their war work. Remember, too, that you can considerably help to relieve overcrowding by avoiding unessential journeys during the busy times

CHARACTERISTIC
NAME PLATE
OF LOCAL OPERATOR

A general poster produced by 'British Buses' for customising by individual operators.

Above: A series commissioned by the popular artist Fougasse who offered his services free to support the war effort.

Left: Almost a 'blackmail' approach to recruitment.

producers in the July edition and by early 1941 there was an increasing emphasis on the wartime effect on manufacturers.

July 1942 typically reflects the times:

Northern Aluminium: now concentrating on war work.
Guy Motors: includes a German endorsement of their products as captured examples in use by the enemy.
Don: emphasises safety in moving war workers.
Crossley: ran a 'Famous Generals' picture series to remind readers that 'Crossley were also leaders!'.

BUT FOR THE BUSES · · ·

The food ship arrives at the port; the dockers get down to the job and another quick turn-round is made.

Speed is the essence of the operation. Moving men from dock to dock, even from port to port, buses have kept labour fluid, to be applied where most urgently needed.

But for the buses, dockside labour could not have been so economically employed.

ISSUED BY THE BRITISH OMNIBUS COMPANIES PUBLIC RELATIONS COMMITTEE
CVS-70

BUT FOR THE BUSES · · ·

The dispersal of factories was simple enough on paper but hedged with practical difficulties which had to be overcome before any progress could be made. Not the least was the transport of workers, first to build and later to man the factories.

It was just another job for the omnibus companies and they took it in their stride.

But for the buses the dispersal of war industry would not have been practical politics.

ISSUED BY THE BRITISH OMNIBUS COMPANIES PUBLIC RELATIONS COMMITTEE
CVS-86

Above left: The British Omnibus Companies Public Relations Committee produced a 'But for the Buses' series of posters highlighting their vital role in supporting other essential activities. This one relates to docks and supplies.

Above right: 'But for the Buses' 2 – Servicing New Factories.

BUT FOR THE BUSES · · ·

The heart of a tank is its engine. Britain's tank designers were lucky to find an industry already in full swing, producing just the engines they required, an industry equipped and experienced to develop the design in the new direction.

You can credit that to the omnibus companies, who fostered the development of the Diesel engine for road transport.

But for the buses our tank designers would have been handicapped before they started.

ISSUED BY THE BRITISH OMNIBUS COMPANIES PUBLIC RELATIONS COMMITTEE

The Buses of Britain

On any average day, the bus companies of Britain provide transport for 12,000,000 passengers — no less than a quarter of the total population of the country. A mighty task, ably performed under the system of free enterprise.

British Omnibus Companies Public Relations Committee.

Above left: 'But for the Buses' 3 – Tank Design.

Above right: A general poster published by The British Omnibus Companies Public Relations Committee.

Redex: 'eases your war worries'.
Sternoclense: 'keeps transport going'.
Oldham Batteries: also a war-related theme.
Sunbeam BTH: use 'home produced fuel'.
HML: gas-producer trailers.
Brush: seeking post-war work.
Bedford: thirty-two-seat wartime bus complete for £825.

However, in the same edition the adverts for MCW, Duple, Metro-Vick and Connolly Leather are unchanged from those used in peacetime.

The magazine itself rarely mentions current UK operations, other than producer-gas problems, but concentrates on features covering overseas fleets and numerous articles suggesting future trends in vehicle design and reorganisation of the industry. In 1945, the 'recent overthrow of Germany' is mentioned and a year later normal practice is resumed with over fifty pages of advertisements in most monthly editions.

UT FOR THE BUSES · · ·

hey've upset a lot of old notions, have the Women's Land Army, as many farmers will admit. There would have been more tightening of belts in Britain if they hadn't. But they presented a transport problem which only the omnibus companies ould solve — transport in rural areas.

But for the buses their splendid effort would have been even more arduous.

ISSUED BY THE BRITISH OMNIBUS COMPANIES PUBLIC RELATIONS COMMITTEE

BUT FOR THE BUSES · · ·

More aircraft . . . more aircraft . . . we must hold supremacy in the air! And we must have dispersal of the aircraft industry, so that enemy attack cannot stem our growing power.

But how to get workers to remote factories? The bus companies have provided the answer — by buses — through blackout, fog, rain and snow; no other means would avail.

But for the buses the soaring heights of aircraft production could not have been reached.

ISSUED BY THE BRITISH OMNIBUS COMPANIES PUBLIC RELATIONS COMMITTEE

Above left: One of a series of advertisements produced on behalf of British Buses to publicise the important role of the bus industry during the war. 'But for the Buses' 4 – Rural Transport.

Above right: 'But for the Buses' 5 – Aircraft Production.

BUT FOR THE BUSES . . .

Miles from the nearest town, a tract of desolate
moorland becomes overnight a scene of lively
activity. Men and machines are changing its face.
Soon a new airfield is on the map.

By the nature of things, airfields are in remote
places. The men who construct them must be
carried long distances to and from their work.

But for the buses, the programme of airfield
development could not have been so ambitious.

BRITISH BUSES

ISSUED BY THE BRITISH OMNIBUS COMPANIES PUBLIC RELATIONS COMMITTEE

Left: 'But for the Buses' 6 – new airfields.

Below: Advertisement for utility Sunbeam trolleybus
– this example was for St Helens Corporation.

*A Sunbeam-BTH Trolley Bus, with
double-deck low bridge type body*

15

Other Aspects of Operations

Finances

As early as September 1939, operators were beginning to worry about the financial implications of wartime operation. An article in *Passenger Transport* (13 September 1939) identified that income had fallen dramatically while overall costs had increased. Income declined as a consequence of service reductions and cancellation of advertising contracts, as suppliers had limited stocks to sell. Expenditure on wages fell as staff left to join the forces, although local authorities tended to continue to pay an allowance to serving personnel. Pay, fuel, electricity and spares costs rose. There was the necessity to provide facilities (shelters, building protection, etc.) in anticipation of air raids and the longer-term consideration as to who would pay for war damage repairs and any costs associated with relocation due to requisition of premises for military purposes. There had also been a net cost associated with the large-scale evacuation of cities as, although rates had been agreed in advance, these had not covered the costs of additional supervision and dilution of revenue elsewhere due to vehicle redeployment. The net result was an increase in revenue per vehicle operated but an increase in both labour costs per mile (due to slower speeds) and standing costs per mile (due to increased overheads and the forced idleness of some vehicles).

The article concluded that most of the industry would soon be in a loss-making position suggesting that it would have to utilise capital reserves. It was suggested that municipal companies could receive a contribution from the general rates; the argument being that in good times transport made a net contribution to local authority funds. It appears that there was no official Government response, if indeed one was sought, but, with hindsight, this scenario proved to be overly pessimistic as circumstances developed to the industry's advantage over the next few years.

Prior to the war a sub-committee had been established to consider how to control the large dividends generated by most major operators as it was intended that they should be part of the Regional Traffic Commissioners' control remit. It was suggested (by 29 January 1942) that the war had increased these profits even though there had been very few fare increases. This was confirmed in individual company results:

1 Ribble's asset value increased by 84 per cent from £2.23 million in 1939 to £4.1 million in 1946, the majority of which was held as cash and government investments.
2 Barton posted 'highest profits ever'.
3 Tilling's 1944 accounts refer to 'excess profits tax' but fail to give any further information other than they expect to recover 20 per cent of it at the end of the war in accordance with Finance Act 1941.

Interestingly, British Electric Traction's accounts for the war years do not reflect any major changes. Possibly this was due to their being a holding company with many other interests outside the UK bus industry.

Vehicle Hirings

Construction, and operation, of airfields and new factories often required operators to source vehicles from elsewhere. However, fluctuating needs throughout the duration of the war saw a considerable number of vehicle loans of which the following were typical:

Cumberland Motor Services: hired vehicles from Manchester Corporation (1940/1); Morecambe Corporation (1942/3); London Transport (1942–4) and Bolton Corporation (1941–6).

Coventry Corporation: (after destruction of tram system in November 1940) used buses from London Transport and seven municipal operators.

Wolverhampton Corporation: hired twelve trolleybuses from Bournemouth Corporation from 1940

In addition to the above, **Manchester Corporation** loaned vehicles to Walsall, South Shields, Derby and Northern Roadways as well as independent operators, Boults, Walsall and Sutton, Kidsgrove. The latter were used 'internally' at ROF Radway Green.

London Transport benefited from the loan of 422 provincial buses during the winter of 1940/1 but later in the war the position was reversed as LT found they had an excess of vehicles that were to be found throughout Britain. Some loans were sufficiently long for them to be painted in the operator's livery.

Throughout the five war years there were many more transfers (probably involving hundreds of vehicles in total), reflecting the fluctuations in demand from area to area and month to month. Often these have not been recorded due to their short-term nature and restrictions in force at the time.

One of the many examples of long-term loans: London Transport ST 631 is seen with Trent. (*OS*)

A wartime view of a United Counties (NV 3146) Tilling Stevens on loan to London Transport in Bromley Market Place. (*OS/EGPM*)

16

Victory Buses

JULY, 1945   Bus & Coach   263

VICTORY BUSES

On *VE-Day* several transport undertakings contributed to their local celebrations by operating specially decorated vehicles.

The *Victory* bus at the top of the page was run for a week by Birmingham City Transport, covering all the municipal routes. The double-decker on the left was used by the Brighton, Hove and District Co. for trips given to local children, South African troops and members of the Hove Old-Age Pensioners' Club, the vehicle being in the charge of Driver Woolgar, a Tilling employee since 1909.

Above is a North Western Road Car Leyland coach and, at bottom left, a Manchester Corporation Leyland Tiger.

Opposite page: Bedford OWBs in a victory parade in Edinburgh to commemorate their role in provision of support services during the war.

Above: A selection of Victory buses.

Post-War Reflections

An address by the director general (Sir Cyril Hurcombe) to the Royal Empire Society on 13 June 1945 entitled 'Transport In War' reflected on the contribution made by road passenger transport during the Second World War. The experiences related were very recent at the time but during the forthcoming years there was little interest in revisiting wartime events by the community at large; hence, the subject was rarely discussed again. The Ministry did sanction an official history, which ultimately materialised as *Inland Transport* by C. I. Savage, but this was compiled from files rather than based on personal experiences.

The main emphasis of the lecture was the changes made to ensure that essential workers were transported while maintaining other services that were vital to the life of the community with minimum resources. This entailed streamlining administration including reorganising the duties of the Traffic Commissioners, giving them greater autonomy as Regional Traffic Commissioners, replacing the licensing procedures (part IV of RTA) with permits and fuel rationing thus allowing 'rapid adjustments to ever changing needs'. They thus had significant involvement in affairs which would previously have been outside their jurisdiction. Planning started before the war with the detailed preparation of evacuation schemes, then followed a policy to ensure there were adequate facilities for vehicle maintenance and repair through designation of essential repair under 'Essential Works Orders' while allowing other premises to be released for use by Minister of Labour and other bodies. Other key responsibilities included giving prior approval for the requisition of vehicles, equipment & premises, the issue of spares and shortage certificates (up to 8,000/week), allocation of new and reconditioned vehicles and determining the fate of any vehicle replaced. On a wider basis they also had to liaise with MoL to ensure sufficient labour was available to meet current transport needs.

The overall objective was to give more direct control of operations to the Minister and thus be able to react quickly to changing circumstances. The reporting structure was revised so that the chairmen of Traffic Commissioners became officers of the Ministry with duty of controlling goods and passenger road transport under Minister's

Savings were encouraged. This (probably) post-war picture of a utility Guy publicises some of Ribble's successes in this area.

direction. These new arrangements became effective immediately on the outbreak of war.

More people were moved over a greater distance than in 1938 including many to 'new' destinations but not without operational difficulties created by vehicle requisitioning in the early days of the war, shortage of new vehicles and severely depleted staff as many joined the Forces and were replaced by women, whose numbers rose from 17,000 (1938) to 80,000 (1945).

Even so, more vehicles operated in 1945 than 1938, passengers travelled longer distances on average and new routes were introduced. Selected statistics indicate 25 per cent more passengers (cf. 1938) but vehicle miles approximately 66 per cent of pre-war levels. This greater efficiency was achieved through a combination of factors and coordination, although some had taken the greater part of the war before they became fully effective. The main ones were staggered working hours, perimeter seating on single-deck vehicles, transfer of road traffic to rail in selected areas, priority travel schemes, regulation of bus queues and stopping places.

A bus well and truly burnt out.

A tramcar silhouetted against the glare of fire.

Almost a direct hit! Note the crater beside the permanent way.

The overhead wires completely demolished by blast.

Top middle: A typical scene of destruction (the "body" happily is only a wax model).

Bottom: Another blast effect—a tramcar body completely removed from truck.

Some wartime casualties.

Appendices

Appendix 1
Explanation of Abbreviations

ARP: Air Raid Precautions
BMMO: Birmingham & Midland Motor Omnibus Company (usually known as 'Midland Red')
CTC: Central Transport Committee
HSG: High Speed Gas Company – a manufacturer of producer-gas equipment
LT: London Transport
M&D: Maidstone & District Motor Services
MoL: Ministry of Labour
MoS: Ministry of Supply
MoT: Ministry of Transport (later Ministry of War Transport)
MoWT: Ministry of War Transport
PG: Producer Gas
PSV: Passenger Service Vehicle
RAF: Royal Air Force
ROF: Royal Ordnance Factory
RTC: Regional Transport Commissioner
SMT: Scottish Motor Traction
TA: Traffic Area
TGWU: Transport & General Workers Union
TNA: The National Archive
UAS: United Automobile Services
Unfrozen: Vehicles built out of parts previously held in store.
Utility: Vehicles built new, to wartime specifications.

Appendix 2
Case Studies of Individual Operators

A Large Coach Operator (Sheffield United Tours)
The primary business was express services and coach tours on which eighty-three coaches were employed. Due to the seasonal nature of the work the majority of the staff were multi-skilled and undertook both driving and maintenance work. The outbreak of war saw an immediate 25 per cent drop in business mainly in long-distance excursions as day trips remained popular throughout the summer of 1940. Following Dunkirk a number of vehicles were requisitioned while others were retained on permanent standby (with drivers) for use by the army. Others were used, on short-term loan, to augment bomb-damaged transport systems in Coventry, Hull and Sheffield. More permanent was the provision of regular troop contracts and daily conveyance of workers in the Sheffield area.

No pleasure traffic was carried in 1941, the vehicles being engaged in transporting construction workers to new airfields and factories, often involving journeys of 40–50 miles from their Sheffield base while others were out-stationed 90 miles distant. All the vehicles showed signs of excessive wear due to arduous duties, bad roads and garaging in the open air. Once the airfields were completed, vehicles were deployed to serve open-cast coal sites and dispersal factories and also to transport Italian prisoners to agricultural and other duties. One specific contract required the movement of 5,000 prisoners in a single night! At the end of 1942 the company was given the opportunity to repurchase some of its vehicles which had been requisitioned by the army but they were amazed at the extremely poor condition to which they had been allowed to deteriorate. (*Source: Bus & Coach, Aug 1945, p.195–8*)

A Rural Bus Operator (Red & White)
The recurring problem throughout the war was the difficulty of matching service provision to demand and resource allocation. The initial requirement to save fuel posed the problem of which services to cut as many were essential to village life and frequencies were low. Accordingly all market-day services were retained. The reductions resulted in surplus staff, most of whom had to be made redundant. Many vehicles were requisitioned but soon released, as they were not of the type preferred by the army.

New factories and aerodromes generated the need for long (often 40-mile) single daily journeys; the increase in population, both as a result of these new facilities and of evacuations to the area, necessitated the reintroduction of services but by this time a labour problem had developed. Older staff had left due to the strains of the blackout, new recruits were often of poor quality resulting in late running and accidents and new female staff 'started under the worst possible conditions'. The Ministry of Labour was demanding better services while at the same time depleting the workforce. The situation was improved by the 'essential work order' prohibiting the transfer of drivers and MoWT representation on the 'Manpower Board' which instigated a degree of cooperation between planning and factory operations.

In common with other operators the vehicles also began to show the consequences of their age and limited maintenance but there were also a few unique problems. One was the fact that curfew times varied in different parts of the company's area creating timetabling difficulties. Another was the (apparently) random allocation of producer-gas vehicles which took no account of their suitability for a company's route network or their ability to maintain the specialised equipment. Such vehicles also posed problems on joint routes for similar reasons. (*Source: Passenger Transport, 11 May 1945, p.273–5*)

A Major Company Operator (East Kent)
Out of the 500-strong fleet, eighty vehicles were requisitioned by the forces and a further 100 used exclusively on Government contract work at locations as far distant as Carlisle and Plymouth. Duties included conveyance of construction workers (in the Midlands) and transport of ENSA entertainers throughout the UK. Substantial damage was inflicted on the Dover area and a number of employees were killed while on duty causing the company to allow those who wished to evacuate the area to do so at their expense. None chose to do so. Despite the problems all services were maintained at 100 per cent except during the period of the Dunkirk evacuation when nearly all the company's vehicles were fully employed for four successive days and nights on troop transportation. (*Source: Bus & Coach, December 1943, p.114–7*)

A posed picture of an SMT Regal showing its potential as an emergency ambulance – the vehicle itself has been equipped accordingly. (*Gavin Booth Collection*)

A Holding Company (Scottish Motor Traction Co. Ltd)
Bus operations were only one of the businesses of Scottish Motor Traction. Their wider interests enabled them to take a more positive approach to the challenges presented by the war, as stated in their post-war review: 'Many months before the company had made tentative and flexible plans with the object of providing the best transport service possible within whatever resources were made available by the government'.

This was achieved despite the loss of men to the Fighting Services, their replacement by untrained women, requisitioning of 9 per cent of the vehicles, shortages of fuel and other resources and significant changes in traffic patterns. During the course of the war the company undertook some PG operations and, like other Scottish operators, had a disproportionate number of single-deckers re-bodied as double-deckers.

The resources of the other sectors of SMT were offered to the Government, who willingly accepted them. The aircraft factory at Airdrie was fully committed to the production of assemblies and components for a succession of aircraft types, while the Car Sales & Service Department was equipped with machine tools, also for the production of aircraft components, but utilising unskilled labour. Initial output was for Hurricane and Blenheim aircraft but these were superseded by those destined for Lancasters. In parallel the company also produced guns, at sites in both Edinburgh and Glasgow, as well as their more traditional vehicle-related activities. In total over 15,000 Army vehicles were assembled; 10,000 separate bodies built; 3,000 trailers; 700 tank transporters plus assorted landing craft and ship components.

Up to 17,000 staff were directly employed on war work, some 2,000 of whom, mainly from the bus operation, were active volunteers in the No. 1 Scottish Home Guard Column. This was established to support the army organisation in the urgent provision of transport. Operating under the direct control of the deputy director of supply and transport, Scottish command, it was capable of providing adequate transport for 20,000 troops within four hours. After it had been stood down it was commemorated in the Parade in Edinburgh on 3 December 1944 with a 'drive-past' of twenty-four troop-carrying buses.

Edinburgh Corporation
As a consequence of a combination of good management, planning and healthy levels of maintenance stores, Edinburgh Corporation had fewer problems than many other operators.

Those trams without headlights were fitted with a cylindrical lamp with red and white shields, similar to that fitted to newer trams. Wiring crossovers were modified to reduce arcing and carbon shoe collectors replaced trolley-wheels. The problem of locating the tram wire at terminal points was eased by fitting of a metal plate which acted as a guide. With the blackout necessitating daytime repairs, trolley wire was replaced by allowing a tram to take current from the 'opposite' wire; obviously there was a requirement to disconnect should an approaching tram wish to pass! Where this procedure was not possible, renewals took place on moonlit nights. By ensuring adequate planning, it was possible to relay track work during the day while still maintaining a service.

Bus services operated to an emergency timetable from November 1939 and finished earlier than hitherto but it was not until July 1940 that the fleet was reduced by the requisition of twenty-five single-deck buses by the War Department, followed by the transfer of coaches a few months later to ambulance and fire service duties. In early 1941 some double-deckers were sent to London as part of the large fleet of provincial buses operated at that time. This scheme was later shown to have been a morale booster rather than an operational necessity. Single-deckers were fitted with perimeter seating to increase capacity and conductresses were recruited in increasing numbers.

New buses comprised a motley collection of double-deckers, with chassis (AEC, Bristol, Guy and Daimler) and bodybuilders (Park Royal, Northern Counties, Pickering, Massey, Brush & Weymann) not previously seen in the fleet. The single-deck fleet was strengthened with two Tilling Stevens, diverted from an order for China; a Bristol L5G; Daimler CO5Gs; plus a number of Bedford OWBs. Again, Willowbrook, Bristol, English Electric and SMT were 'new' bodybuilders. Despite this diverse selection there were no significant problems in procuring (or making) spare parts to keep them running.

As elsewhere, Edinburgh was reluctant to convert vehicles to producer gas; nine did operate between April 1943 and October 1944 but the lack of power was an obvious drawback.

It did not take long for operations to return to normal after May 1945. Lighting was restored, masks and white paint were removed and all vehicles were painted into fleet livery. The overall assessment was that 'the tramcar and bus fleets had been maintained to near-normal standards'. (*Source: Hunter p60–70*)

Douglas Corporation

The introduction of changed procedures to comply with wartime restrictions caused minimal problems to Douglas Corporation, thanks to judicious pre-planning. The necessary blackout materials had been procured in advance so that all vehicles were fitted in a single day. Evening services were curtailed as part of an overall policy to reduce fuel requirements. This resulted in a 'surplus of labour' but rather than forcibly reduce the staff, the union agreed to a 'sharing of work'.

As in other places, financial matters were a problem in the early days as it was difficult to see how the extra expenditure on security and building modifications would be recouped; so great was the preoccupation with this matter that it generated twelve sets of reports, three sets of budget forecasts and thirty-six committee meetings! However, after a fare increase and a 22 per cent passenger increase (due to restrictions on car use) the problem solved itself. Further savings were made by converting six vehicles to one-man operation and the sale of used tickets 'for salvage'.

A unique consequence was that all horse trams had to be withdrawn, for the duration, due to the erection of barriers along the Promenade. (*Source: Bus & Coach September 1943*)

Liverpool Corporation

Despite a fair amount of pre-planning, being a large organisation it took a while for Liverpool Corporation operations to adapt to wartime conditions. By mid-1939 the erection of shelters, employee protection and camouflage of buildings was well advanced but work on the fleet was frustrated by the 'ever changing regulations' re vehicle lighting and associated blackout requirements. Window netting was fitted to all trams and buses. Until late October 1939 it was deemed unsafe to maintain services during 'alerts' as the use of headlights was forbidden. There had also been a judicious increase in fuel stockholding in the months before war was declared.

It was decreed that normal bus mileage should be restricted to 60 per cent of the 1938/9 level and that duplication should cease on tram routes but major problems arose with the need to service new factories at Speke and in the East Lancs Road area. Although fuel was made available, vehicle utilisation was very low due to the peak one-way flows and long layovers. Initially vehicles were hired in for this traffic but later, a special fleet of eighty-four ex-London Transport double-deckers was purchased (at less than £100 each). The tramway was also extended to cope with the huge demand – a side effect was that the local press stopped their constant demands to 'scrap the trams'!

Despite these extra demands the motor bus account moved from a £70k loss pre-war to £37k profit due to the additional traffic, a reduction in wages, speed restrictions and the employment of female staff. (*Source: Passenger Transport 13/12/40*)

Wolverhampton Corporation
The following extract is one of the few observations showing the detailed changes in bus operations as the war progressed. Similar actions must have been replicated elsewhere but neither the local records nor RTC instructions that gave rise to them have survived.

1938/9 Preparations for War:
The Council established a general committee to oversee all the corporation's responsibilities re Government (National Emergency) requirements
In accordance with ARP instructions all glass roofs and lighting to be screened
In March 1939 permission given for MOT to requisition ten single deck buses for conversion to ambulances (ten stretchers per vehicle) – these passed later to Ministry of Health with the corporation supplying drivers. 4 were later returned but had to be kept available at 4 hours notice
Air raid shelters constructed at depots and fire pumps purchased, first aid classes provided
Staff encouraged to join the Territorial Army – those who joined Regular Forces continued to be paid (less monies received from Military)
Initial blackout trials on buses proved unsatisfactory to the police – subsequently used Birmingham system
A conflict arose between the requirement for fuel saving and need for additional services to local aircraft factory

1939
Services curtailed after 2200hrs from 10 September 1939 resulting in complaints leading to 1 late journey on each route

Agreement was given to purchase a year's supply of spares in advance

1940/1
Drivers could continue after age sixty-five
Women paid same rate/hour as men but restricted to 40hrs/week
A 20 seat bus was made available to Home Guard and subsequently sold to ARP
The transport set up Local defence Volunteers squad comprising 150 men
Crews were given discretion as to whether to proceed during air raids
Permission to extend the trolleybuses to the aircraft factory was refused due to 'likelihood of flashes' – ultimately permission was given by which time traction poles were unavailable
Following the bombing of Coventry two buses were lent to Daimler Company
By March 1941 wartime financial problems resulted in request for a fares increase which was refused
Dispersed vehicle parking introduce to limit damage to vehicles in air raids
Longer hours of evening operation refused by RTC
Accommodation was leased to provide a canteen and rest room for female employees

1943
Three daily journeys provided to a new Ordnance Factory outside the town but this was later handed over to private operators
Number of bus stops reduced in accordance with 'Queuing Order' directive
RTC request for space at bus garages (for Factory & Storage Department) was refused as some already used by Guy Motors and Civil Defence
A new order was given by RTC to further reduce services, due rubber shortage, from January
Inconsistencies continued as trolleybuses ran later than buses as the former were not subject to RTC authority
It was noted that annual usage had increased from 70 million (1940/1) to 88 million (1942/3) and the RTC sanctioned a 1 per cent increase in provision

1944/5
To overcome shortages, bus drivers were allocated by Ministry of Labour but as these took precedent over existing conductors, the latter had to be paid at driver rates for all duties.
From November 1944 late journey restrictions lifted but difficult to provide as Transport department was short of 122 personnel by this date.

First Days of Peace
VE Day 8/9 May were national holidays – all staff received full pay (on 8th) plus enhancements for those actually working
Difficulty was experienced in releasing staff from Armed Forces as transport was not seen to be a priority; hence, impossible to meet increased demand for services in the short term. (*Source: A History of Wolverhampton, Vol. 2, P. Addenbrooke*)

A Journalist's Perspective

John Parke, speaking to a meeting of the Omnibus Society in October 1945, highlighted a number of aspects of wartime operations. Primary among these was the problem of achieving adequate interior lighting during 'blackout conditions'. Initially torches had been utilised but as the war progressed more ingenious solutions were introduced. The national companies used a moveable lamp sliding along a batten fixed to the roof above the gangway which the conductor slid along (using an attached handle) as he issued tickets. When Southdown fitted their open-top vehicle with temporary roofs, they incorporated old ashtrays into which a bulb was fitted horizontally with a metal deflector plate above it, thus achieving an adequate light in which to issue tickets.

Vehicle appearance suffered during the war years with light roofs painted over in dark colours (which varied according to availability of supplies); fleet names were excluded by some operators due to local defence requirements but there was no general rule in this respect. Destination displays also varied between locations to reflect views of local officialdom but when invasion seemed a possibility many buses merely displayed 'blank' or 'relief'. A consequence of this was the need for operators, who had previously not done so, to introduce a system of route numbering.

Other consequences of wartime were the reduction in the number of bus stops, introduction of compulsory queuing orders and the requirement for operators to provide shelters where relevant, such as outside factories. To assist in this, the Regional Traffic Commissioners had powers to override any objections the local authorities may have regarding their siting. Elsewhere the local authorities were expected to provide queuing rails, with the MoWT having powers to enforce this.

Appendix 3
Wartime Legislation Schedule

Reference	Date	Title

Defence (General) Regulations (1939)

Reference	Date	Title
1197/39	01/09/1939	Railway Control Order
	15/09/1939	Road Vehicle & Drivers Order
1406/39	26/09/1939	Standing Passengers Order (1939)
1296/39	27/09/1939	Compensation (Defence)
1398/39	29/09/1939	Drawing of PG Trailers Order (1939)
1544/39		Control of Noise Order
1676/39	09/11/1939	Local Authorities PSV Order (1939)
1720/39	21/11/1939	Standing Vehicles Order
55/40	15/01/1940	Petroleum (No. 1) Order (1940)
74/40	19/01/1940	Lighting (Restrictions) Order (1940)
101/40	27/01/1940	Built up Areas Order
107/40	29/01/1940	Interest on Compensation (Defence)
370/40		Staggering of Working Hours
376/40		Mutual Aid Schemes
396/40	08/07/1940	Standing Vehicles Order Amendment
594/40	16/04/1940	Standing Passengers Order (Trolley Vehicles) (1940)
583/40	17/04/1940	Amendment
741/40	06/05/1940	Road Vehicles & Drivers Order (1940)

781/40		Control of Employment Under Defence Regulations
826/40	28/05/1940	Motor Fuel Rationing (No. 2) Order
841/40	28/05/1940	Petroleum (No. 2) Order (1940)
962/40	01/06/1940	Petroleum (No. 3) Order (1940)
1007/40	18/06/1940	Removal of Direction Signs
1055/40	26/06/1940	Motor Vehicles (Control) Immobilisation
1299/40	01/07/1940	Traffic on Highways
1305/40		Conditions of Employment Order
1328/470		Removal of Licence Disqualification
1352/40	11/07/1940	Acquisition and Disposal of Motor Vehicles
1377/40	30/07/1940	Removal of Direction Signs (No. 2)
	31/07/1940	Road Vehicle and Drivers Order (1st Amendment)
1496/40	11/08/1940	Road Vehicles (Prohibition of Camouflage)
	1563/40	Road Vehicles (Prohibition of Camouflage) Amendment
1677/40	19/09/1940	Fire Watches Order
1730/40	23/09/1940	Amendment (No. 2) Order
1797/40	15/08/1940	Traffic Commissioners (Redn of Nos) (1940)
1826/40		Suspension of Driving Tests
	10/08/1940	Formation of Queues Order
	19/08/1940	Standing Passengers Order (Perimeter Seating)
	29/09/1940	Road Vehicle & Drivers Order (2nd Amendment)
1872/40	23/10/1940	Amendment (No. 2) Order (Lighting)
1882/40	13/07/1940	RTC (Restriction of Movement)
2018/40	21/11/1940	Amendment (No. 3) Order (Lighting)
2097/40	21/11/1940	Amendment (No. 3) Order
8/41		Mutual Aid Schemes
25/41		Staggering of Working Hours
89/41		Mutual Aid Schemes
108/41		School Buses
116/41		Fuel Rationing – PSVs
279/41		Perimeter Seating
286/41		Abolition of Basic Fuel Ration
366/41		Perimeter Seating
368/41		Registration for Employment Order
398/41		Construction and Use
402/41		Closing Times of Cinemas/Theatres
426/41		Staggering, Bus Shelters, Queue Control
447/41		Central Transport Committee Scheme
541/41		PSV Conditions of Fitness
625/41		Amendment Order (Lighting)
643/41		PSV Equipment and Use
963/41		Acquisition of Vehicles
1425/41		Lighting
1680/41		Standing Passengers (No. 2) Order
1884/41		Conditions of Employment Order (Amendment)
1998/41		Immobilisation of Vehicles
2104/41		Standing Passengers (No. 3) Order
2127/41		Motor Fuel Rationing
2128/41		Motor Fuel Rationing
2/42		Standing Passengers Amendment Order No. 2
3/42		Recruitment of Conductresses
8/42	01/01/1942	Acquisition and Disposal of Motor Vehicles (1942)
40/42		Unattended Vehicles
93/42		Recruitment of Conductresses
126/42		Upgrading of Drivers
151/42		Part Time Labour
189/42		Abolition of Basic Fuel Ration
221/42		Upgrading and Dilution of Drivers
337/42		Regulation of Traffic (Formation of Queues) No. 2 Order
390/42		Local Consultancy Schemes

398/42		Transfer of Conductresses
452/42		Sunday and Late Night Services
464/42		Preference in Recruitment of Conductresses
465/42		Transfer of Conductresses
838/42		Acquisition of Vehicles
1073/42		Conditions of Employment Order (Amendment)
1535/42		Permit in Lieu of PSV Licence
1594/42		Essential Work (General Provision) (No. 2) Order
1678/42	15/08/1942	Acquisition and Disposal of Motor Vehicles (2nd Amendment)
1691/42		Reg. of Traffic (Formation of Queues) (No. 2) Order
2400/42		Control of Motor Fuel Order
2533/42		Motor Vehicles (Restriction of Use) (No. 2)
2673/42		Conditions of Employment No. 2 Order
49/43		Queue Barriers and Markings
53/43		Road Vehicles (Functional and Other Marks)
142/43		Employment of Women Order
166/43		Strengthening of Bus Services
176/43		Strengthening of Bus Services
316/43		Lighting
651/43		Control of Employment (Directed Persons) Order
771/43		Immobilisation of Vehicles

Additional Legislation:

Gen6	1/43	Supply of Conductresses
Gen22	10/43	Supply of Conductresses
Gen29	06/01/1944	Preferences in Labour Allocation
Gen1	26/01/1944	Preferences in Labour Allocation
		Curtailment of Express Services
		Vehicle Interior Lighting
		Requisition of Premises
		Producer Gas

In additional to this, all existing previous legislation was also in force.

Appendix 4
Wartime Calendar

March 1937	Committee of Imperial Defence first address wartime policy
1938	Emergency Division of MOT established
Summer 1938	Pre-planning meetings (Ministry and industry)
October 1938	Munich Crisis
April 1939	Traffic Commissioners instructed to prepare fuel saving schedules
31 August 1939	Introduction of control schemes
31 August 1939	Cessation of Green Line services
1 September 1939	Start of vehicle lighting restrictions (Blackout)
3 September 1939	War Declared
September 1939	Amended lighting regulations (no off-side headlights)
September 1939	Mass Evacuations of Cities
16 September 1939	Original date for fuel rationing
23 September 1939	Actual date of fuel rationing
October 1939	Further revision of lighting regulations (off-side headlights ONLY)
January 1940	Urban speed limit reduced to 20 mph
22 January 1940	Compulsory headlight masks (either!)
1 June 1940	Evacuation of South-East England
9 June 1940	RTC orders cessation of Tyne-Tees-Mersey services
20 July 1940	Order controlling purchase and control of motor vehicles

1940	MOT organises vehicle loans to London, Coventry and Bristol
Autumn 1940	Increase in fuel allocation
15 October 1940	Scheme for ex-military vehicles to return to original manufacturer
End 1940	Reduction in fuel allocations
1 February 1941	Bus driving becomes 'Reserved Occupation'
Early 1941	Problems identified in Potteries
Early 1941	War Office agree to release of 900 vehicles (at 200 per month)
1 March 1941	Concerns re new vehicles and spares
Early 1941	Rootes Committee organises maintenance and spares
April 1941	Reduction in bus and coach services
April 1941	Liquid gas trailer production commences
1941	Problems identified in South Wales
1941	War Office released about 280 vehicles (47=scrap)
April 1941	War Transport Council formed
1 May 1941	MOWT established
1941	Select Committee foresees major transport problems in winter of 1941/2
September 1941	Articulated bus demonstrated in Liverpool
15 September 1941	Two masked headlights permitted
Summer 1941	Severe restrictions on recreational services
October 1941	First Utility bus demonstrated
October 1941	Twelve standees permitted and perimeter seating
December 1941	Bedford OWB shown to MOS – 1,200 ordered
1 January 1942	Acquisition and Disposal of Motor Vehicles Order introduced
1 January 1942	Army lend 420 coaches for civilian use
1942	Further restrictions on use of fuel and tyres
1 September 1942	Abolition of basic ration for PSVs – all fuel via RTC
1 September 1942	All non-essential coach services suspended
1 October 1942	All remaining express services cease (Government order)
Late 1942	Directive to convert 10 per cent of large fleets (over 150) to liquid PG
29 September 1942	All Green Line services withdrawn
June 1944	London Evacuation (V Bombs)
Summer 1944	Increase in fuel allowance – off peak services resume
November 1944	All services reinstated (except Sunday and long-distance)
25 April 1945	End of Blackout Regulations
1 June 1945	Recommencement of cross-country express services
26 June 1945	Leisure travel permitted up to 70 miles
6 February 1946	First Green Line services recommence
11 February 1946	Discontinuance of necessity for purchase licence
March 1946	Victoria Coach station reopened
14 April 1946	Restrictions on leisure travel lifted

Appendix 5
1942 Census Extracts

MOWT: Summary of all operators of 20 vehicles or more

Region	no of operators	ambulances	military	TOTAL s/d under 32 excding amb etc	licenced	licenced maxm per day	not licenced repair	not licenced surplus
1 NORTHERN	12	36	1	193	127	114	33	33
2 NORTH EASTERN	23	79	40	376	241	210	20	115
3 NORTH MIDLAND	19	34	5	364	316	285	21	27
4 EASTERN	8	75	6	457	369	360	47	41
5 LONDON	15	327	403	437	406	323	29	2
6 SOUTHERN	17	67	1	386	329	285	10	47
7 SOUTH WESTERN	9	42	1	825	671	323	66	88
8 WALES	19	12	7	196	156	124	37	3
8 A NORTH WALES	1			14	13	13	1	
9 MIDLAND	17	59	133	290	245	193	43	2
10 NORTH WESTERN	40	97	21	1414	1339	942	23	52
11 SOUTHERN SCOTLAND	18	106		432	314	184	76	42
11B NORTHERN SCOTLAND	4	3		32	29	26	3	
12 SOUTH EASTERN	6	88		243	180	147	2	61
	208	1025	618	5659	4735	3529	411	513
UNITED AUTOMOBILE SERVICES LTD		11	1	128	78	74	21	23
RIBBLE		16	0	417	417	166	0	0

TOTAL s/d over 32 exclding amb etc	licenced	licenced maxm per day	not licenced repair	not licenced surplus	Double Decker excl ambulce etc	licenced	licenced maxm per day	not licenced repair	not licenced surplus
1218	1120	1057	65	33	473	460	445	13	
1216	1154	1054	31	31	1535	1490	1389	31	14
1017	952	864	18	47	922	906	840	16	
371	311	300	49	11	506	456	438	50	
817	774	731	24	19	4772	4745	4375	26	1
448	422	388	21	5	729	689	652	17	5
870	794	440	63	13	968	924	861	64	
1058	971	869	63	24	604	568	524	31	3
9	9	9							
1451	1406	1253	43	2	2025	1985	1821	39	1
1292	1245	1107	27	20	3866	3730	3392	121	15
2014	1786	846	213	15	1514	1412	889	96	6
86	82	76	4		106	101	98	5	
518	490	467	9	19	708	681	656	27	
12385	11516	9461	630	239	18728	18147	16380	536	45
659	592	557	34	23	94	92	88	2	0
243	243	178	0	0	295	295	265	0	0

Appendix 6
'The South Wales Solution'

By 1943 the MoWT was becoming increasingly concerned that all buses should be used as efficiently as possible. In August a report from the local RTC suggested that this was not the case in three areas of South Wales.

Maesteg–Caerau: This 2.5-mile route with a 15–20 minute frequency was worked by five separate operators as per the following:

	Mon – Thurs (20 minutes)	Fri/Sat (15 minutes)	Sunday (20 minutes)
30-seater	3	7	3
20-seater	3	3	3
14-seater	1	1	1

However, due to the complexity of the schedule some vehicles were only used two days per week with the result that the capacity offered differed from day to day. The MoWT told operators to make the service more economical and fix the daily number of seats. After some negotiation Mrs Brewer acquired the services of the other four and provided a service exclusively with thirty-seat (or above) vehicles – four on Mon–Thurs, six on Fri/Sat and three on Sunday.

Local Barry Services comprised a seven-mile network provided by five one-vehicle operators plus three Western Welsh giving a combined five-minute frequency. There was no incentive to improve efficiency as each of the five owners was content to maintain the status quo.

The RTC considered that a combined service would reduce the number of buses to four. Accordingly, the private operators were informed by the Manpower Board that better use of labour was required and there would be no objection to any operator or driver being called up! The file lists all the individuals and their vehicles as a first step to action but the authorities were not prepared to go any further 'in case they set a precedent'.

J. Williams (aged 45) two thirty-seaters (one out of use); 50 miles/day-stage and workers services; one driver (46) – 6.5 hours/day.
A. Williams (36) one thirty-two-seater, 50 miles/day-stage and workers; one driver (39) – 6.5 hours/day.
A. Morgan (57) one thirty-two-seater; 50 miles-stage; one driver (32) – 6.5 hours/day.
R. Guppy (40) one thirty-seater; 50 miles-stage, one driver (32) – 6.5 hours/day.
A. Walters (deceased) one thirty-two-seater; 50 miles-stage, one driver (38) – 6.5 miles/day, service operated on temporary licence by executors.

Aberavon–Pontrhydfen: another 2.5-mile route but with ten operators and twelve vehicles providing a frequency of 20 minutes (Mon.–Fri.), 10 minutes (Sat.) and 30 minutes (Sun.).

Full operator details were:

E. A. Jenkins (39) PSV driver, no employees.
David Jones & Son (49) PSV driver, nine s/d vehicles (of which two on stage and seven on workmen's services), ten drivers (ages given).
William Jones (61) no PSV licence, one s/d, one driver (39); no other services.
Joseph Mason & Son (43) PSV, one s/d; only service.
E. A. Stephens (41) PSV, one s/d; only service.
Thomas Bros Ltd – I. D. Evans (43), Secretary. No PSV, ten s/d (two on stage), nine drivers. Also operates other stage and workmen's services.
Theolphilus Thomas (59) PSV, one s/d, only service.
John Williams (51) PSV, one s/d, only service.
Rhyd Lewis (49) PSV, one s/d, only service.
W J Clement (46) PSV, one s/d, only service.

After prolonged negotiation operators were reduced to three by takeovers:

Thomas Bros acquired Clement, Theo Thomas, J. Williams & Mrs E. A. Stephens.
P. Jones acquired Mrs E. A. Jenkins.
Rhyd Lewis and W. Jones created a partnership and acquired J. Mason & Son
The vehicle requirement was reduced to four (Mon–Fri), three (Sat) and two (Sun).
(*Source: MT55/257*)

Appendix 7
London Evacuation Plan Dated 27 September 1938
Compiled by H. H. Piggott – Regional Traffic Commissioner

The initial detailed plan for the evacuation of children from London commenced as early as September 1938 and was continually revised over the succeeding twelve months. An extant file (in Lewes) indicates the degree of involvement by bus operators.

The plan overseen by Mr H. Piggott (the Southern RTC) envisaged a two-day process with 100 trains each day to various Southern stations, with similar numbers to other SE destinations. It included the number of evacuees to each railhead, the requirement on individual bus companies, and how many people were allocated to each District Council.

Approximately half a million people required transport:

Destination station	Bus Company	Numbers
Bletchley	United Counties	11,700
Wolverton	United Counties	18,200
Aylesbury	Eastern National	14,200
Princes Risborough	Thames Valley	10,800
Maidenhead	Thames Valley	18,300
Henley	Thames Valley	9,700
Reading	Thames Valley and Reading Corporation	14,100
Pangbourne	Thames Valley	4,000
Radley	City of Oxford	11,300
Chosley	Thames Valley	5,850
Wantage Road	City of Oxford	7,800
Uffington	City of Oxford	4,800
Newbury	Newbury & District	10,700
Thatcham	Newbury & District	5,200
Theale	Thames Valley	3,000
Hungerford	Newbury & District	3,000
Basingstoke	Venture	11,400
Andover	Wilts & Dorset	10,700
Culham	City of Oxford	6,650
Witney	City of Oxford	8,250
Oxford	City of Oxford	4,200
Chipping Norton	City of Oxford	6,950
Kudlington	City of Oxford	1,700
Banbury	BMMO	6,000
Bicester	City of Oxford	4,200
East Grinstead	Southdown	19,300
Uckfield	Southdown	20,000
Brighton	Brighton & Hove/Brighton Corporation	27,500
Hove	Brighton & Hove	23,500
Portslade	Brighton & Hove	2,800
Southwick	Southdown	3,800
Shoreham	Southdown	6,100
Newhaven	Southdown	2,000
Hastings	Maidstone & District	35,000
Bexhill	Maidstone & District	11,100
Rye	East Kent	6,300
Battle	Maidstone & District	5,700
Seaford	Southdown	2,650
Worthing	Southdown	56,650
Eastbourne	Eastbourne Corporation	24,200
Polegate	Southdown	11,350
Littlehampton	Southdown	6,400
Arundel	Southdown	1,050
Bognor	Southdown	15,700
Chichester	Southdown	32,650
Horsham	Southdown	17,600
Haywards Heath	Southdown	7,500
Total:		551,550

Once they had all been relocated there was an additional need for the bus companies to transport the children to local schools and provide access to shops, etc. for the increased population.

Appendix 8:
Manchester Corporation Perimeter Seating

Very little of the correspondence between Regional Traffic Commissioners and individual operators has survived. The following file relates to the introduction of perimeter seating by Manchester Corporation and is reproduced in its entirety to give an idea as to the level of detail discussed. Similar correspondence must have existed on many subjects between all RTCs and local bus operators. (*Source: North Western Traffic Area file CM1/C14*)

MCTD to RTC, 25 September 1941
In conformity with Passenger Road Services Standing Passengers Order 1941, seating being altered in single-deck buses to permit additional standing room.

CM1/24	West Didsbury–Droylsden
CM1/17	Levenshulme–Eccles
CM1/75	Chorlton–Eccles
CM1/155	Oldham Road, Newton Heath–Fallowfield
CM1/202	Heaton Park–Hollinwood

MCTD to RTC, 18 October 1941
Negotiations with T&GW who suggested increased number be permitted only on services to and from works during the rush periods. In view of the fact that almost the entire fleet of single-deck buses have been converted and the inconvenience of having different regulations at different times on different routes agreement reached that the maximum number of standing passengers at any time should be twenty.

Meeting, 30 October 1941, RTC, DPO and two T&GW reps
RTC neither approved or disapproved of the agreement. T&GW preferred to carry twelve on ordinary buses. Mr Thomas (T&GW) outlined the discussions which had taken place with MCTD leading to the limit of twenty standing passengers in reseated single-deckers.

MCTD to RTC, 7 November 1941
49 buses converted to date. Not proposed to convert any more at the moment.

MCTD to RTC, 8 November 1941
The Standing Passengers (No. 2) Order 1941: one half of the seating capacity of single-deckers or the lower saloon of a double-deck bus or a maximum of twelve be allowed to stand.
    Request that conditions apply to whole of services.

RTC to MCTD, 13 November 1941
Review of general sanction. Why not "movable notice" to secure the maximum fluidity in working the vehicles on services?

VE reported 14 Nov 1941 that the Assistant Bus Superintendent had told him that all vehicles on which the seating arrangement had been altered are to be altered back to the original positions.

MCTD to RTC, 15 November 1941
Idea [in 13 Nov 41 letter] 'presents considerable difficulty'.

Report of Inspector C. Copestake, Thursday 20 November 1941, Eccles service
Guards – No body support during the collection of fares causing them to fall on to the knees of sitting passengers. Passengers' knees and feet when spread out, which they often are, make walking down the bus difficult and dangerous. More fatigued when finishing duty. Delay in collection of fares caused by standing passengers because they are nervous of releasing their hold of the hanging strap to obtain from their purse or handbag their fare.

Passengers – The lack of body support when standing. Inability when standing to use both hands to obtain fare from purse or handbag and the fear of finding oneself sitting on somebody's knee, and the thought of being stared at and looked over through sitting face to face.

Report of Inspector T. E. Lawless, Thursday 20 November 1941, Service 19 Droylsden–West Didsbury

1. The danger of accidents to passengers increasing owing to being unable to hold on to any support when rising from seats.
2. When carrying twenty, standing passengers find that many have a tendency to crowd into space near the emergency door, thus causing congestion at a place which, in my opinion, is undesirable.
3. This type of seating definitely causes much longer delay at stopping places while passengers board and alight.
4. Is not approved by travelling public.
5. Transverse seating with an increased number of passengers standing would be more appreciated both by crews working buses and passengers.

Report of Inspector Williams, Thursday 20 November 1941, Service 19
I found that the average number of standing passengers carried by conductresses and guards on this service, even during rush hours, is twelve, this number enabling them to collect the fares in comparative comfort.

On one or two occasions when this number was exceeded by a further two or three passengers the difficulty of negotiating the standing passengers became apparent. Passengers appeared to be loathe to move from the position they occupied on account of only having hanging straps for support, whereas previously they had supported themselves against the seats which form the gangway or aisle.

When there were no standing passengers fares seemed to be collected more quickly and the movement of guards and conductresses appeared to be more free.

The majority also appear to agree that the maximum number of passengers for a minimum of comfort during collection is twelve.

Conductress: 'It causes more trouble through passengers being over carried as they will wait until the bus is on top of the stop before making an attempt to leave their seat.'

MCTD to RTC, 21 November 1941

Refers to meeting held with the other operators with inter-running arrangements regarding 12 standing.

Memo RT Divn to RTC, 23 December 1941

Refers to phone message sent Saturday 13 December to the effect that reconversion should be stopped at once. Our transport resources are likely to be strained to the utmost in the coming months ... The Minister is disturbed at the apparent lack of progress which is being made on conversion [this is assumed to be a general observation]. Manchester Corporation cannot be allowed to reconvert but it may be that an improvement could be effected by the transfer of converted buses to more suitable routes.

Circulars 279/41 [dated 27 August 1941] and 366/41 indicate in general terms the types of routes and services on which these buses should be employed ... If there is still a surplus of converted buses belonging to the corporation you should make arrangements for transferring such vehicles to other routes and services in your region, if necessary on a exchange basis.

If experience shows that to allow thirty standing passengers makes travelling impossibly difficult you may like to consider reducing the vehicles somewhat on specified routes or services.

Asks for report in the near future on progress as regards to the question generally in your region.

Mr Shallice phoned 24 Nov 1941 regarding report received from one of our VEs. All except twenty-five had been altered. These twenty-five were to be used solely at rush hours on the services authorised for their use.

MCTD to RTC, 24 November 1941

Had converted 49. "These buses have been operated on Droyslden route." Not liked by the conductors nor is it popular with the public. Enclosed inspector's reports.

I am forced to the conclusion that this type of seating is only suitable in the main for munitions workers and similar kinds of traffic. In these circumstances I propose to revert back to the transverse type of seating on all except twenty-three buses which we will keep for special kinds of traffic.

In some districts I understand that uprights have been fixed for supports but these appear to interfere with the conductors' work.

RTC to MCTD, 25 November 1941

The RTC notes owing to the circumstances referred to you propose to revert back to the transverse type of seating on all except twenty-three vehicles.

'The reports of your plain clothes inspectors are very interesting and the facts are being reported to the Minister of War Transport.'

RTC to Assistant Secretary, Road Transport Division, Berkeley Square House, 1 January 1942

Forwarding memorandum received from MCTD. You will appreciate that Manchester Corporation in converted all their single-deckers went beyond what your circular 279/41 dated 27 Aug 41 evidently envisaged. You will remember that your fifth para stated:

•   It is considered that buses adapted as indicated should be used primarily on factory services
•   where there are heavy peak loads in preference to ordinary town services.

The Corporation now intend to conform to these. They have tried conversion on ordinary town service and have found it quite unsuccessful for the reasons given. That being so they are now restricting the use of the converted buses to the peak time workpeople's services you had in mind when your circular was drafted. The T&GW take strong exception to their unrestricted use on all day long ordinary town services. The number of standing passengers has already been reduced to twenty by arrangement between the Corporation and the T&GW.

You will see from the Corporation's memo that the reconversion of that portion of the fleet which was scheduled for reconversion has already been practically converted and there seems little point in holding it up. The Corporation ought not to be penalised because in their anxiety to be helpful they went further in conversion than the Minister expected and experience warranted.

RT Division (Birtchnell) to RTC, 22 January 1942

While the Corporation may have used converted buses on services for which they were not wholly suitable it is presumed that the routes in question were approved by you for operation with such buses and the Minister finds some difficulty in understanding whey the converted buses were not transferred to more suitable services. The retention of only twenty-three converted buses appears to him to be a very small number for an undertaking of the size and importance to industry of Manchester Corporation Transport.

I agree that in the circumstances there is no point in holding up the completion of reconversion of that proportion of the fleet which was wrongly scheduled for conversion.

The Minister is not satisfied with the present progress as regarding conversion and wishes more energetic action taken. I hope that you are bringing pressure to bear on all undertakings operating on routes and services which seem to you to be suitable to convert to the maximum number of buses.

RTC to Assistant Secretary, Road Transport Division, 30 January 1942
MCTD to RTC, 13 July 1942

We are operating the converted buses on the following services:

19 West Didsbury and Droylsden
22 Levenshulme and Eccles
23 Chorlton and Eccles
67 Newton Heath and Fallowfield
56 Heaton Park and Holllinwood
- Victoria Station–London Road Station (Forces bus)

Converted buses: 25, 58, 63/6/7, 75/6/9, 81–5/7/8, 95/6/9, 126–30 (23)

Not converted: 23, 36/7, 47–51, 60–2/4/5/8–74/7/8, 80/6/9–94/7/8, 131–7/4–8

MCTD to RTC, 19 October 1943
We do not propose to alter any more buses from transverse to longitudinal seating largely due to the opposition of the trades unions.

A scene that highlights the effect of the War on vehicle supply. Ribble was unable to obtain Leyland vehicles; hence, the presence of these Daimlers at Lancaster in grey livery. The Duple bodied example (ACK755) and the Brush (ACK 777) have differing indicator layouts, neither of which adheres to the company's standard. (*S. N. Poole*)

Bibliography and Sources

Files at TNA (mainly MT55 & MT56 series)
Transport World
Bus & Coach
Passenger Transport
Commercial Motor
PSV Circle publications
MTA Journal

General Histories

Hay, I., *The Story of The Royal Ordnance Factories 1938–1948* (London: HMSO 1949)
Hibbs, J., *The History of British Bus Services* (Newton Abbot: David & Charles 1989)
HMSO, *Transport Goes To War* (London: HMSO 1942)
Klapper, C. F., *The Golden Age of Buses* (London: Routledge & Kegan Paul 1978)
Savage, C. I., *Inland Transport* (London: HMSO/Longman 1957)
Tilling Group, *The War That Went on Wheels* (Bradford: Autobus Review 1978) reprint of 1945 publication
Townsin, A., *The Best of British Buses No. 8 (Utilities)* (Glossop: Transport Publishing Company 1983)

Specific Bus Companies

Addenbrooke, P., *A History of Wolverhampton Transport Vol. 2* (Droitwich Spa: Birmingham Transport Historical Group, 1995)
Akehurst, L., *Green Line* (Harrow: Capital Transport, 2005)

Carter, P., *Premier Travel Ltd* (London: Capital Transport, 1995)
Eyre, M. and C. Heaps, *The Manchester Bus* (Glossop: TPC, 1989)
Graves, C., *London Transport at War 1939–45* (New Malden: Almark, 1974)
Holmes, P., *Thames Valley* (Glossop: TPC, 1984)
Howie, J. D., *Ribble in Wartime* (Ribble Enthusiasts Club: 2010)
Hunter, D. L. G., *Edinburgh's Transport – The Corporation Years* (Adam Gordon, 1999)
Kraemer-Johnson and J. Bishop, *Glory Days – East Kent* (Ian Allan, 2005)
Lacey, P., *Thames Valley*
Maund, T. B., *Ribble*, (Glossop: Venture Publications, 1993)
Newman, A. G., *London's Wartime Gas Buses*, (Capital Transport, 1997)
Oxley, A., *Midland General* (Robin Hood, 1999)
Postlethwaite, H., *Cumberland* (Glossop: Venture Publications, 1996)
Powell-Hendry, R., *The Omnibus 1940–1980*, (Rugby: Hillside, 1982?)
Prince, J., *Glory Days – Hants & Dorset* (Ian Allan, 2006)
Scottish Motor Traction Co. Ltd., *A Short History of the Company 1905–1945* (SMT, 1946)
Senior, J. A. and J. Banks, *The Weymann Story* (Glossop: Venture, 2002)
Telfer, R. L., *Stratford Blue* (Stroud: Tempus, 2003)
Watts, E., *Fares Please – History of Passenger Transport in Portsmouth* (Portsmouth: Milestone, 1987)

Area Transport Histories

Baker and Robbins, *A History of London Transport Vol. 2 – The 20th Century to 1970* (London: George Allen & Unwin, 1974)
Horne, J. B. & T. B. Maund, *Liverpool Transport Vol. 4 (1939–1957)* (Glossop: Transport Publishing Company, 1989)

Acknowledgements and Photographs

I wish to express my gratitude to the many fellow enthusiasts who have assisted me in the collection of material. Prominent among them are Alan Lambert and Tony Newman who have made available the fruits of their researches in TNA files, thus saving me the effort of doing it all again! Ken Swallow and the late Wilf Dodds provided valuable input of both information and advice, as did Gavin Booth and Mike Sutcliffe. Alan Mills and Alan Oxley found me everything in the Omnibus Library that related to the Second World War and the PSV Circle publications were essential in 'decoding' what I found. Derek Hedger read the early drafts and offered his continual support. Primary thanks must, however, go to the people and organisations who compiled the original source material and kept it secure for so many years.

Most of the photographs are from three collections held by the Omnibus Society: John Parke (OS/JFP), Charles Klapper (OS/CFK) and Douglas Spray (OS/DHDS). Others are from my own collection. Apologies are offered for the poor quality of some as wartime restrictions limited photography by amateurs and many of those that do exist reflect the quality of materials available. Original professional views have proved difficult to locate; hence, in some cases, I have had to resort to reproducing some of them from trade magazines, the quality of which deteriorated as the war progressed.

20/02/ 2013

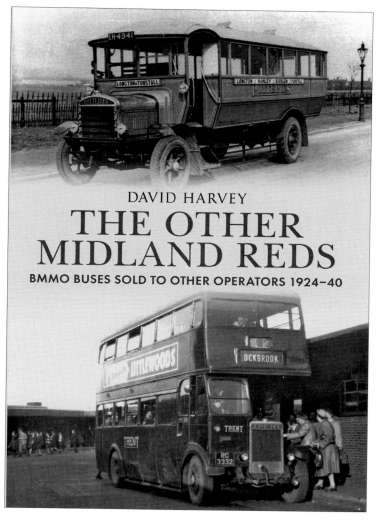

The Other Midland Reds

David Harvey

The history of Midlands buses from 1924 to 1940, illustrated with many previously unpublished images.

978 1 4456 1329 1

160 pages

Available from all good bookshops or order direct
from our website www.amberleybooks.com

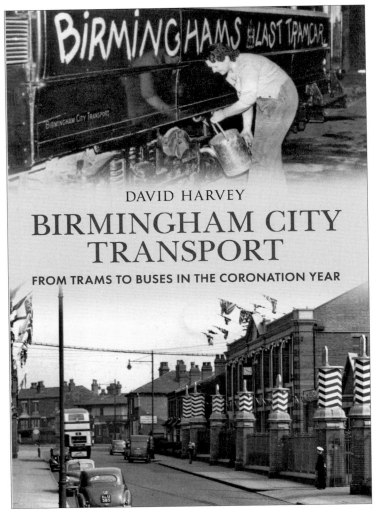

DAVID HARVEY

BIRMINGHAM CITY TRANSPORT

FROM TRAMS TO BUSES IN THE CORONATION YEAR

Birmingham City Transport
From Trams to Buses in the Coronation Year
David Harvey

This fascinating selection of photographs gives an insight into
Birmingham and its transport in the Coronation year as the city's
last tramways closed.

978 1 4456 1496 0
160 pages

Available from all good bookshops or order direct
from our website www.amberleybooks.com